on track

The Incredible String Band

every album, every song

Tim Moon

sonicbondpublishing.com

Sonicbond Publishing Limited
www.sonicbondpublishing.co.uk
Email: info@sonicbondpublishing.co.uk

First Published in the United Kingdom 2021
First Published in the United States 2021

British Library Cataloguing in Publication Data:
A Catalogue record for this book is available from the British Library

Copyright Tim Moon 2021

ISBN 978-1-78952-107-8

Typeset in ITC Garamond & ITC Avant Garde
Printed and bound in England

Graphic design and typesetting: Full Moon Media

on track ...

The Incredible String Band

every album, every song

Tim Moon

sonicbondpublishing.com

Would you like to write for Sonicbond Publishing?

We are mainly a music publisher, but we also occasionally publish in other genres including film and television. At Sonicbond Publishing we are always on the look-out for authors, particularly for our two main series, On Track and Decades.

Mixing fact with in depth analysis, the On Track series examines the entire recorded work of a particular musical artist or group. All genres are considered from easy listening and jazz to 60s soul to 90s pop, via rock and metal.

The Decades series singles out a particular decade in an artist or group's history and focuses on that decade in more detail than may be allowed in the On Track series.

While professional writing experience would, of course, be an advantage, the most important qualification is to have real enthusiasm and knowledge of your subject. First-time authors are welcomed, but the ability to write well in English is essential.

Sonicbond Publishing has distribution throughout Europe and North America, and all our books are also published in E-book form. Authors will be paid a royalty based on sales of their book. Further details about our books are available from www.sonicbondpublishing.com. To contact us, complete the contact form there or email info@sonicbondpublishing.co.uk

on track ...

The Incredible Sting band

Contents

We're All Still Here; No One Has Gone Away

Robin Williamson and Mike Heron: whatever the ups and downs of the band, these two Scottish gentlemen were the constant. In fact, to some extent, it hardly mattered who else was alongside – if they were there, it was The Incredible String Band. From that initial phase as a trio with Clive Palmer, through the dancing hippie chicks Mimi and Mouse, the steady introduction of the girlfriends as members – Christina McKecknie, better known as Licorice or Licky, and Rose Simpson, better known as, well, Rose – through to the dancer, Malcolm Le Maistre, and the steady introduction of various members as the rock element grew, it was always Mike and Robin at the core – writing and singing, separate and yet a unit. Robin, with his fey and mystical songs, exploring philosophy, religion and mythology, in a grab bag of parts that somehow made immediate sense as a whole. Mike – slightly more grounded but complimentary – the perfect foil, adding the songs with a kazoo and an acoustic guitar, to sing to that girl with the long hair that you'd finally enticed back to your halls of residence. Start with 'Log Cabin' and end on a version of 'Rainbow', and she would be yours. Maybe.

The band had begun as a duo of Robin Williamson and Clive Palmer, not under the ISB name, but as Beatniks. The hippie label was not yet coined. They lived a beatnik existence in the flats of Edinburgh, sharing the life with the likes of Bert Jansch. Hard-living, floorboards were burnt to keep warm, and when all that could burn was burnt, a tent was erected in the middle of the floor for some relief from the biting Scottish winter – so cold that smoke froze solid. Apparently.

Robin and Clive played the clubs and sessions, doing traditional folk and old-time American banjo tunes. They were getting a name as great players: Clive and his banjo, Robin and his fiddle, and the guitars. Growing fish in a growing ocean. Mike had encountered them as he made his way around the Edinburgh music scene, toting his guitar. See Mikes autobiographical book, *You Know What You Could Be*, for full details on this period, but suffice to say, the two added the one, Clive's Incredible Folk Club gave them a name, and they were off and running; The Incredible String Band. Now the name has connotations beyond its origins, reflecting the old-timey basis. Enter Joe Boyd – musical whizz-kid about town. His portfolio has included Fairport Convention, John Martyn and Nick Drake – in fact, a who's who of folk rock royalty, and that aside from Pink Floyd, Jimi Hendrix, and others from that side of the folk/rock wall. So when he encountered the trio, he was impressed, installed them in a studio, recorded a debut album and got them a deal with the cool American Elektra label.

There will be more about the albums in this book, of course, but at this point, things go a little awry as Clive heads off to Afghanistan and Robin scoots off to Morocco, neither planning to return anytime soon, if at all. Mike continues to play solo around Scotland and misses his comrades. Clive leaves the picture, but before long, Robin returns to the nest, bearing a suntan and much more: crucially, a number of ethnic instruments, including that key ISB sound, the bowed gimbri. Actually, Robin decided to bow it, but most Moroccans played it as one would a mandolin. In a veritable aviary of pleasure, the robin and the heron reconvened, and the String Band was back in business as a duo, ready to take on the world with a run of eccentric but breathtaking albums. Perhaps it's best to pause here to point out that the albums were indeed breathtaking, but a matter of taste. Few are indifferent: you either adore them with a passion or scream, 'For god's sake, turn that off', within 30 seconds.

The dancers, Mimi and Mouse, came and went, and the duo set about the seminal *The 5000 Spirits or the Layers of the Onion*, followed by *The Hangman's Beautiful Daughter* and *Wee Tam and The Big Huge*. Licorice and Rose Simpson – the girlfriends and fellow travellers – cropped up on the odd track, singing, beaming from the album sleeve, or contributing an instrument. And all this time, the perfume of a certain brand of herbal cigarette, mingled with even more mind-bending items, to present another world which we mere mortals could only wonder at.

But change was afoot, in the form of Scientology – a cult-like belief system – and to illustrate the removal from external to internal influence, the next album was entitled *Changing Horses*, and behold, as the two girls became official members, the band was now a quartet. For many, it seemed like the magic was diminishing, as this album and its follow up, *I Looked Up*, were not as well-received as that initial run. Frankly, these are still very good albums but were just not able to easily follow what went before.

The band had even managed to play at Woodstock without ever getting to appear in the film or on a soundtrack record until the 21st century!

Next, the foursome decided to take a multimedia step, developing a largely inexplicable stage show – or a 'surreal parable in song and dance' – using the talents of a hippie dance troupe called Stone Monkey. The resulting show and album, called simply *U*, lost money hand over fist, though the double album has magical music scattered across its grooves.

A move to the Island label – where virtually all of Joe Boyd's Witchseason Productions artistes resided – saw a slightly inconsequential album and a fascinating, if dated, film, called *Be Glad For The Song Has No Ending*. Part-documentary, part-hippie-silent-movie, it was to be the last outing for Rose Simpson, as she departed out of sight, only to re-emerge as 'the hippy who played at Woodstock, now the Lady Mayoress of Aberystwyth'. Well, it was a good headline.

Rose's replacement was one of the dancers, Malcolm Le Maistre, who had sung on a track on the *U* album. It made sense. Rose was, in her own opinion, not a musician, but within the band was given fiddle and bass guitar parts to play. Malcolm could equally not play, but mandolins and clarinets were thrust into his hands, and he got his head down and learned.

The first Island album with this line-up – the charmingly titled *Liquid Acrobat as Regards the Air* – showed that the band retained much magic, alongside a growing rock influence, which was further developed on the next album, *Earthspan*. But it was time for a change, as Licorice departed 'for a break', though that break continues to this day. Indeed, her whereabouts remain a mystery, and amidst much speculation, many assume her to be no longer of this world. This time, in came a replacement in the form of a studious young reeds and keyboard player named Gerard Dott: friend of Mike, and about as likely a new recruit as signing up Alice Cooper to Take That. The one album with this line-up, *No Ruinous Feud*, shocked the fans with its slick cover, soft rock feel, and even a Dolly Parton song. Exit Gerard.

There was one final album to go, as the band expanded with a full-time drummer – one-time roadie, Jack Ingrams – Stan Schnier as full-time bass and steel guitar player, and the splendid rock guitar of Graham Forbes. It was fairly short-lived, and the album, *Hard Rope & Silken Twine*, showed a band that was pulling itself in two directions: Mike looking to the commercial rock side, Robin looking to return to the more simple acoustic musings. A new album was started but never finished, tracks from it appearing on Mike's post-ISB offering, *Mike Heron's Reputation*. Mike continued to explore the rock aspect with his band(s) before taking a step back and re-emerging with The Incredible Acoustic Band, which did what it said on the tin. Today, Mike is something of an icon and sings much of his old ISB catalogue, perhaps at last at peace with his heritage.

Meanwhile, Robin had moved to America with his wife Janet Shankman and steadily set about exploring his Celtic roots, most obviously with his Merry Band: all harps and bagpipes, an area that he continued to explore on subsequent solo albums. After moving back to the UK with his new wife, Bina, he's settled into a Celtic bard role, becoming an accomplished storyteller, using the harp as his primary instrument and producing an amazing run of albums, including guitar albums for the cool ECM label.

The Incredible String Band were a bookmark in musical history. But then, out of the blue, Mike, Robin and his wife Bina reformed the band in the 21st century, along with that long-gone original, Clive Palmer, who Robin had recorded and toured with.

Mike and Robin had done a couple of concerts as a duo, carefully not using the ISB name. It was said they reformed to refute Joe Boyd's claim that they never got on. But the new ISB didn't last long – Robin didn't want to coast on nostalgia, while Mike wanted to present the old songs to a new audience. So Robin left, and Mike and Clive carried on, producing live albums of the old songs, before putting it to rest once again.

Before we look at those albums from the years 1966 to 1974 (and the 21st-century recordings), we have to mention the instrumentation. If the band had a USP (unique selling proposition), it was the huge array of usual and unusual instruments they used. Mike moved from being 'just' the guitarist, to adding the fashionable Indian instrument, the sitar, to his armoury. Of the two, Mike was more the solid base, adding keyboards regularly and sometimes harmonica, bass and electric guitars, with occasional forays into other items. Robin, meanwhile, leapt from the starting point of guitar and fiddle, adding flutes and whistles, the bowed gimbri (of course) and then anything which came to hand and fitted with the music he wanted. Hundreds of instrumental credits litter the albums.

So, that's about as thumbnail as it can get. For further information, consult the horse's mouths, as Rose has an autobiography on her time with the band, published, and Mike is working on the second volume of his memoirs, which will, no doubt, pick up where the first left off, just prior to *5000 Spirits*.

But let's pick up on some of the major lines of thought above and take a closer look at the 'Marmite Theory'. For the String Band, there seemed to be no barriers, no area out of bounds. If it was played anywhere in the world, well, let's listen, absorb and add to the mix. 'Does that make a sound? Yes. Well, I'll play that for twelve bars in that song and never pick it up again.' I'll talk more about the instruments later. But we live in a world where, if somebody tells you such and such a band are 'really different', you can bet that they mean they sound pretty much like a million other bands, but with a slight twist. Bob Dylan (purportedly) said, 'As a songwriter, you should listen to nobody or everybody', and no wiser words have been said. We've all encountered the band in the pub that only take half a song for you to know exactly which band they have listened to above any others. Years ago, I entered the *Melody Maker* Folk and Rock Contest and watched as a fellow entrant plugged his acoustic into an Echoplex and proceeded to not only play exactly like John Martyn but even do an accurate impersonation of his voice to introduce the numbers. He probably makes a living as a tribute act these days. Anyway, this never seemed to plague Robin and Mike. If they listened to Ravi Shankar, they listened to American doo-wop. If they listened to Chinese musicians, they listened to Robert Johnson (the blues one, not the one with Steeleye Span – do keep up. And whosoever they listened to, they blended it into a fascinating mix, even within the same song. Even on the heavily folk-influenced first album, the signs were there. Dylan-esque American singer-songwriter styles rubbed shoulders with Scottish folk tunes, while minstrel-style old-time banjo tunes tipped a wink to very British pastoral influences. For many, it was all too much: they wanted to pop the vinyl down and hear Paul offering to drive your car, then staying on the main roads until the destination.

I often muse that if the band started today, would they be anywhere near as big as they were? More than ever, the record business want a clear marketing angle. And while I don't say Mike would be back in the solicitor's office within six months, I can't help but think that they would be filed away under 'eccentric cult band', whose albums would be released independently, the band covering the costs. But who knows in the game of 'what if'? Certainly, my time operating computers on the night shift in the early 1970s, saw others screaming when I played ISB in the rest room. And for me, all strength to the band for following their own path and not deviating. Some may say that in their latter years – post-Scientology and on the Island label – they did follow the route of fame and commercial success. But listening to the albums now, even 'that' wasn't fully the case. *No Ruinous Feud* wasn't Led Zeppelin, and it wasn't even Chicory Tip – it was still the ISB behind the electric guitars, because, look, here a whistle and organ number, here a sitar, there an oud. Still not easy on the casual listener.

Which, rather neatly, brings us to the ISB's USP. Err, yes. And that is instrumentation. We live in a world where if the guitarist so much as taps a tambourine, he/she is lauded as an extraordinary multi-instrumentalist. But the ISB took that to a whole other level. Robin was the chief instigator of this, but nobody was free of it, and until the final rock band years, everyone was cajoled into different spheres of instrumentation. For Robin – coming from the folk scene – this was probably a natural thing. In that scene, most people play, at the very least, a couple of instruments. In Fairport Convention for example, Richard Thompson's stunning guitar work was augmented by his playing the piano accordion, and later, whistle, hurdy-gurdy, mandolin and much more. Even Simon Nicol played fiddle and dulcimer alongside his guitar, bass and synth. No self-respecting guitarist was complete without a bag of harmonicas; no fiddler was short of a mandolin, and so on. But the folk scene – in particular the traditional side that Robin was part of – was a pretty open affair, at least instrument-wise, more than the standard pop band line-up that was exotic if it had a keyboard or sax player. It would be a wonder if Robin had only been a fiddler. But the discerning ear can pick up, even then, the outside influence of Clive on Robin's playing – his fiddle on the first album jig owes as much to Kentucky as Kilmarnock.

So, on that first album, the band's instruments reflect the folk scene standard: acoustic guitars, fiddle, whistle, flute, banjo etc. This was to change as Robin returned with the gimbri. While he could have played those opening notes to 'Chinese White' on the fiddle, the eerie drone of the African instrument added something so exotic and tantalising that it may as well have come from another planet. But this was just the start, and on albums two and three, new instruments appeared. In some cases, other musicians were brought in. Mike played none of the sitar of *5000 Spirits*, Dolly Collins played flute organ, and Danny Thompson played double bass (neither of which appear to have been played by the band subsequently), but much of the basis was still guitar, or, increasingly, piano and organ, with Robin usually adding the flute, fiddle and whistle flourishes. And yet, the sound they made still didn't sound conventional. Robin's oud (a fretless North African lute) was played, but often he would use the low melodic runs characteristic of the oud in his guitar-playing. He still does to the day.

Meanwhile, Mike was handling keyboards, and by album three had developed a strong ability on the sitar: the large gourd-bodied Indian instrument whose sound is familiar to anyone who has enjoyed a curry in Britain. It is said that Robin gave him the instrument because he wanted Mike to have more to do than just be a guitarist, but that may just be hearsay. Whatever, it's easy to underestimate Mike's ability on the instrument, perhaps because he was just one more in the post-George-Harrison scrabble to add sitar to any song you could. Mike had a beautifully flowing style, and it's sad that he gradually ceased playing it, though it did reappear on the final ISB album, and I have fond memories of Mike playing it at Preston Guild Hall. As Mike was the lesser multi-instrumentalist, it's as well to add here that on occasions in the recordings, he played flute, mandolin and a few other bits and pieces alongside the guitars and keys. Robin, meanwhile, had said in an interview that you didn't need to know how to play an instrument; you just needed enough knowledge to play the right notes for a particular song that needed the colour of the instrument's sound. It was a theory he tirelessly pursued over the years, and to a lesser extent, still does. I once had a jocular conversation with Robin, in which I pointed out that any back problems I developed in later life from lugging massive numbers of instruments onstage would be entirely his fault.

Perhaps I should elaborate a little on the instruments mentioned so far. As a musician, it's easy to forget that my knowledge is a little better than most on such matters. The main African instruments Robin returned with were the oud and gimbri. The oud resembles the lute that you tend to see in historical films where the minstrel gently croons in a corner. It has a bowl-shaped back and is about two foot in length to the base of the neck, with the sound hole often having carved, decorative shapes. The neck is about another foot long and resembles a violin, as there are no frets (the strips across the neck) such as you find on a guitar. The strings are of nylon or gut, and there are five. It plays a melody line rather than a strummed chord.

The gimbri is an ethnic instrument of the same family, but much smaller, roughly the size of a violin, but with only two strings, and is played with a plectrum. Robin, for whatever reason, got a double bass bow and played it with that. The sound was mesmerising. Sadly, Robin's disappeared: according to him, eaten by rats.

But back to the plot, as it were. *Wee Tam and the Big Huge* saw little new entering the fray, though Likky plays Celtic harp on one track. Her playing seems to be limited to running down the strings, albeit very effectively. The Celtic harp is smaller than the concert harp (think Harpo Marx for one of those), and has nylon strings. The strings play a scale as per the notes on a piano, and you know where C and F are by those strings being red and blue, respectively. It's the first appearance of what would become Robin's chief instrument after the ISB: initially played alongside him by Sylvia Woods in the Merry Band, but then by Robin himself in his subsequent solo career.

The album also saw the bass guitar arriving as the band's first electric instrument, excluding the electric organ. With *Changing Horses*, electricity continued, as the opening song had the twanging of the electric guitar. History doesn't recall any major cries of 'Judas!' at their gigs, and it's probable that their ability to play larger venues meant they could use the louder version of the acoustic guitars without drowning out the others. This was the album where Rose and Licky became proper members: Rose primarily now the in-house bass guitarist, and Licky, the organist, though both would play other instruments as required. But this album shows the ISB dictum of using the instrument that suits, even if it's a one-off. The Chinese banjo, for example, appears here only. Like any instrument that has banjo in its name, its body is – rather like a drum – a tight skin stretched across a circular frame, giving a much sharper, more brittle sound than a wooden box body.

The vibraphone also makes its only appearance here, and you wonder if it just happened to be in the studio and they decided to use it. Essentially, it's a sophisticated glockenspiel – the metal bars arranged like a piano keyboard are struck with soft ball-ended sticks. Air is blown and controlled under the pipes, giving the haunting, ringing, sustained notes.

The standard drum kit had appeared before but was played in a quite basic way amongst the myriad of percussion the band employed. But by the time of *I Looked Up*, there's the first appearance of a real drum kit sound, courtesy of Fairport Convention's Dave Mattacks. Rose recalls with wonder the pleasure she got from playing bass against Mattacks' spot-on time-keeping.

There was also the appearance of the hammer dulcimer. They are effectively rather like a small piano, where the player strikes the strings with soft hammers rather than pressing keys for the same effect. They appear in many cultures under different names: cymbalon in Hungary; santoor in India etc.

There was more India on the *U* album, as Robin played the shehnai: an Indian wind instrument where the reed is in a chamber rather than lipped; its loud rasping tones being ideal for outside events. When Malcolm Le Maistre joined, he was taught instruments as needed. Though strangely, as he was Rose's direct replacement, he did play bass guitar. But he did play clarinet, predating the appearance of the instrument alongside saxophones when Gerard Dott joined. By this stage, the more band-orientated format meant the introduction of new exotica took a back seat. There were only small variations: for example, Robin's alto flute – a deeper and larger version of the normal one – or his homemade electric cello. In fact, the only major new instrument to the fold was after the reformation, when Clive would play his small handmade pipes: bagpipes with a gentler sound blown by air from a bellow worked by the player's arm. Hopefully, all this will give some insight into the sounds you hear, but there's plenty to find online if you wish to know more.

Many have wondered about Mike and Robin's background and unlike modern celebrity culture. it was, for a long time, very vague. Of course, with both Mike and Rose having published autobiographies, we have more background information. Robin, however, remains quite vague. He was brought up in Edinburgh – this much we know – but I think he prefers to keep things a little obscure. He is a lovely man to interview and chat to, but sometimes it feels as though he only says the parts you want to hear about. It doesn't help that his autobiographical songwriting often isn't. A case in point is his post-ISB song, 'Mad Girl'. Now, anyone who has seen a picture of him close-up will have spotted the remnants of a scar on his cheek. In the song, Robin plays truant, and as he rambles, he meets a mad girl. He feels akin to her and moves toward her, at which point she picks up a piece of flint and flings it hard at him, creating a gash on his cheek. 'You took me for an enemy/And I took you for a friend'. So there was the explanation for the scar. Except, talking to him later, he claimed the song was fiction. But was it?

Finally, in this introduction, we must, at least briefly, address Scientology. Now, the 1960s and early 1970s was the period when every self-respecting musician would seek enlightenment, and following The Beatles, it was a case of looking East: the Fab Four with the Maharishi, Pete Townshend with Meher Baba, and so on. And there were certainly elements of this in ISB lyrics: Krishna would pop along regularly, and the Christian god would also make himself known, alongside Maya and other more obscure religious icons. But with the ISB, the feeling that 'all will be one' hung on, as all the religions seemed to be in the band's melting pot of belief. Until Scientology. Joe Boyd blames himself for the conversion, as you can read in his autobiography *White Bicycles*. He took the ISB to meet a guy who was offering the answers through Scientology. Joe himself was unconvinced and walked away. Not so the ISB, who saw it as a light ahead. Scientology was founded by an American named L. Ron Hubbard (early copies of *Earthspan* have 'All strength to LRH' in the sleeve notes). LRH was an author, and his initial concept was of a set of ideas for therapeutic purposes. But by the early 1950s, he relaunched his ideas as a religion. The core belief is that humans are immortal spiritual beings, known as Thetans. Scientology's aim was to make its followers more open and successful. So the little hippie band saw greater things ahead and signed up. It must be noted that Scientology has changed over the years: now it is considered by many as an extremely controlling and subversive organisation, more often considered a cult than a religion. Indeed the US government often investigates its actions. But it was less so when the band signed up, by all accounts. Initially, there was little change in the band's music. Oh yes, there were songs that referred directly to the beliefs, but if you weren't aware, you would likely not have known. Even the overt 'Seagull' from *Earthspan* could be about any experience on the sea.

But as the 1970s rolled on, the band edged closer to a more commercial presentation, the hippie drag becoming velvets and crisp shirts. And drums and bass and electric guitars saw them occasionally being mobbed by teenyboppers. Scientology had brought its change. But rather like The Beatles and Allen Klein, the more business-like approach also sealed its fate, with an increasingly uncomfortable-looking Robin. In the end, the band split, with him heading away with Janet Williamson (nee Shankman) to America, where he became a reborn Celtic acoustic bard with his Merry Band.

Of the others band members, well, read Rose's splendid book for her side; Licky – the beatnik girl from Edinburgh with a spirit so free – is missing, unexplained; Malcolm Le Maistre – often unfairly blamed for the falling fortunes of the band – continues to create music and community drama in Scotland; Gerard Dott plays in trad jazz bands, and Graham Forbes writes great books and still spanks a mean plank in all manner of bands including a Rolling Stones tribute.

So, please enjoy the words that follow, but remember: these are my views and yours may be different, and that's how it should be, really. To all of you, may the long time sun shine on you.

The Incredible String Band (1966)

Personnel:
Mike Heron: vocals, acoustic guitar
Robin Williamson: vocals, violin, acoustic guitar, whistle, mandolin
Clive Palmer: banjo, acoustic guitar, vocal, kazoo
John Wood: engineer
Joe Boyd: producer for Witchseason Productions, sleeve photographer
Record label: Elektra
Release date: September 1966
Chart position: UK: 34
Running time: 45:07
Current Edition: Available on various labels, including a budget reissue of the first five albums.

And here it begins. The wee lads from Scotland launch their recording careers, with an album which features at least two all-time classic songs, alongside a further fourteen tracks which never disappoint. Back then, it all seemed strange and eclectic, whereas now, well, it still seems strange and eclectic. Here were three people who were finding music that wasn't blasting out from Radio One, nor, to be strictly accurate, from the BBC Light Programme: Tony Blackburn was over twelve months from launching the poptastic BBC station.
So let's start with the cover. The military Pepper man was yet to brighten our world, so we basically get a black cover, with those late 1950s/early-1960s graphics: thin red lines like spotlight beams drawn by a kid discovering a ruler for the first time. Bottom left, intersecting lines hint at a fretboard, but only hint. The band name sits at the top, all in lower case, and using the sort of font popular with shoe shops of the time for their' with it' signs. To the left of that, a red line outlined in yellow separates it from the names of the band in white upper case. And in the middle, there is the band. The Incredible band. And they are all holding stringed instruments — the Incredible String Band. Ah, now I get it. The trio are not in the order of the printed names, and I suspect – or rather I know – that a good number of buyers spent some time thinking that Clive was Robin and Robin was Clive. Ah well, that would shortly sort itself out in a fairly drastic way. They appear to be in a stockroom or a library with shelves of documents, and the instruments must be some of the handful that never appeared on an ISB record. Clive grasps a one-string teardrop-shaped instrument, maybe some kind of gadulka or the like. Robin holds a squared-off triangular instrument, possibly bowed, and like a smaller homemade cello. Mike has a large multi-strung instrument, almost circular, and using the sort of tuning pegs used on autoharps and the like. The American release and some of the CD reissues feature the three clambering on a bus lying on its side in a scrapyard. Mike looks a little groovier with his mum's fur coat and a small skull cap. I like the original best. You choose.

Clive looks pale, his red hair not falling like the sky but clean and brushed. He wears beige trousers, a brown check work shirt and, bizarrely, tops it off with a shiny black oilskin coat. Robin sports the beard and short hair with a fringe that the cool kids sported and wears a broad-necked cotton shirt with vertical stripes. Mike looks impossibly young and wears a crisp white shirt, such as a lad who works in an office might wear. Mind, at the time, he 'was' a lad who worked in an office.

The album came out in September 1966, after being recorded at Sound Techniques studios in Chelsea, London – a task that took just one day in May of that year, the album clocking in at a little over 45 minutes, which was a decent length for the time. It was Joe Boyd who pressed them to write their own material for the album and for each to sing their own material. This left Clive at something of a disadvantage, and the outcome of that is that the band are only a band on three tracks, with no less than nine of the sixteen tracks being solo efforts and a further four being duets.

On the back of the sleeve, Mike penned a fey little tale of the band being animals floating down a river on logs – which just about stays to the right side of twee – and he gave a jokey little summary of each track, along with who plays what, which was not always the case back then. On release, there was a good showing for a debut album, being voted Folk Album of the Year by *Melody Maker*: one of the weekly music papers that have now disappeared. It didn't chart, though, as is often the way, when the later album, *The Hangman's Beautiful Daughter*, went top 5 in 1968, the debut did reach 34.

Listening now, the album still has many merits. Simpler by far than what was to follow, and with pretty straightforward instrumentation, the songs are left to fend for themselves on their melodic merits, and they never disappoint in that department. It has a real charm all of its own, and if I was to criticise at all, it would be on the level of wishing there was more interplay. It would be good if Clive's banjo was on that, or Robin's fiddle played there – but it's nitpicking. Mostly I just marvel at how mature the band sound, given this was Robin's first crack at writing.

Is this the album to introduce new ears to? Well, it's certainly a little more accessible than later works. It's definitely the closest to folk the band ever were, though, coming from out of the folk clubs, there is little surprise there. In an alternative reality – where Joe Boyd never told him to write – it's conceivable that Robin would have been another great Scottish traditional player. Or maybe not – what was inside him would surely have found an outlet in due course. In this context, the instrumentals already seem like a throwback to a past life, though jigs and reels would continue to appear throughout the band's existence and beyond in Robin's case. Only Clive's old-time banjo tune – with its unfortunate title for modern ears – came back in the revived 21st-century band.

So, this opening salvo is one to come back to, listen to with ears open to the period in which it's set, and continue to marvel at the talents that were already coming through.

'Maybe Someday' (Heron)

And we are off. And at a canter too, Robins fiddle cracking on at a pace, the minor key adding to the feel of a gipsy stomp. At the time, most of us were unaware of much of the world's music. Some cool cats listened to Indian sitars, but for the most part, our ears were attuned to the 4/4 musings of popular beat combos. So hearing such a time signature played on a scratchy violin really made your ears prick up. Sure as hell, this wasn't Gerry and the Pacemakers! It's said that the band at the time would buy cheap and obscure LPs of all manner of music from around the globe and listen intently. And it seems likely that a middle-class lad from Edinburgh can only have got this stuff from such a source. Mike himself – for it is he – has an assured and rhythmic guitar, underpinning Robin's fiddle pyrotechnics, and his voice enters to tell of his quest to find the perfect woman, who is proving elusive. There are charming lines that throw a curve-ball at the narrative – 'The one she chose, I did not like the way her teeth grew', being one such. As a taster for eclectic tastes to come, this was as good a start as any.

The song essentially hangs on an A minor. Minors being sad-sounding, it provides a wonderful counterpoint to the sprightly tune and occasionally comedic lyrics.

'October Song' (Williamson)

If you were to start writing songs, you'd expect a few false starts: the stumbles as your legs limber up before you start to run. With Robin, this wasn't to be. His first attempt produced this total classic of a song: praised by the likes of Bob Dylan and John Lennon and regularly covered by musicians to this day. Robin takes it solo, just his voice and a mature bit of acoustic guitar. You're forced to muse at the lick-swapping interplay between himself and flatmate Bert Jansch. This was a wonder from the off, and the beginning of Robin's guitar style, showing as time went by, the kind of playing that is more akin to the oud. But that was to come – here it's clean and crisp. And the lyrics were that rare thing: the poetry that works as song lyrics. You could pick any number of lines to quote, or you could sit cross-legged and work out what hidden meaning was there, man. Who is the man whose name is time? What is the door behind the eyes? In the end, like any song, it's what you want it to be, but with not a word out of place. Robin had hit the ground running, and there was much more to come.

'When The Music Starts To Play' (Heron)

Back to Mike, and back to the duo format, with Robin taking up the whistle and opening with a sort of unrelated whistle tune before the happy little song gets into its stride. The interplay between voices is a fascinating aspect of the String Band – but on paper, not a good mix. Mike has a very straight-ahead tone for most of the time – a precise vocal styling. Robin, on the other hand, has a voice which soars and creates insane harmonies, swooping up to falsetto and down to a rich baritone. This interplay of the disparate voices would develop, but already – three tracks in – it was showing itself, and the wonder was that it, somehow, worked. Mike's song is from his heart and honest. Indeed his life had been a 'short one' to this point, but already he knew it was heading in one direction, and it wasn't as a be-suited clerk. When the music started to play, his heart soared, high. And you know what? So did mine and many others!

'Schaeffers Jig' (Trad. Arr. Palmer/Williamson)

Another duo track, and one which almost certainly harks back to the pre-Mike folk club duo days. Short and sweet, there seems little reason why Mike wasn't added, to push it along with some solid guitar chords. But it's left to Robin to do some nimble fiddle, and Clive to play in unison on the banjo. It's a workmanlike bit of tune-playing, but here seems to be little more than an interlude.

'Womankind' (Williamson)

Having got the bit between his teeth, Robin seemed to have little difficulty developing his songwriting. We are in early hippie days, so the song lyric explores the woman as a mystical goddess of love, a philosophy that was gaining prevalence. And yet, is it just me, or is their a hint of a young bloke wanting to get laid? Well, perhaps, but there's no denying the song's beauty, or the unusually complex guitar structure. It is the second Robin solo on the album.

At this stage, Robin's guitar-playing was in the finger-picking style, which a number of players had developed from blues and ragtime, and I don't doubt that sharing accommodation with Bert Jansch formed part of Robin's development in this respect. Although it was an accomplished method, Robin would later develop the oud-playing-influenced style that he made his distinctive own.

'The Tree' (Heron)

Now it's Mike solo, guitar and voice. It's one of the songs that would reappear in re-recorded form later in the band's career, on *Liquid Acrobat as Regards the Air*. Thanks to Mikes book, we can now confirm it was a real tree that he would visit for contemplation and indeed solace. The line about the world being 'endless gloom' refers to the increasingly stifling office job that had been keeping the wolf from the door. It's a song that is at once simple and complex and shows the path Mike's writing was taking. Unlike in some bands, the two writers seemed to plough their own paths, yet added their own characteristics come performance time.

It's an interesting exercise to compare the two versions of 'Tree'. Here, the acoustic guitar provides a more than adequate backing. But when placed next to the *Liquid Acrobat* version from not many years later, the song's true merit comes out, with its between-verse weight. But more of that in due course.

'Whistle Tune' (Trad. Arr. Williamson)

Robin blows a pleasant whistle tune and blows it well, as you would imagine. But like the jig, it somehow smacks of the last wisps of what went before and provides another interlude. It's interesting that no title is attributed to this track. While players often know tunes, if not titles (I'm guilty of that myself), it's often possible to find the title if you're recording, and given all the session players in 1960s Edinburgh, there must have been somebody who knew. Pre-internet and all that, but still...

'Dandelion Blues' (Williamson)

Americana from Robin, with Mike there too. A lovely little ragtime blues, with a feel like one of those songs that you write thinking, 'This feels like a song that'll work with a folk club audience'. Well, with its chorus of 'I do believe it's easy', it feels like that, while the lyrics are a trifle Dylan-esque, chatty and not too deep. Bob Dylan, having emerged in the early 1960s, was a huge influence for change in the British folk scene. Introspection was now leading the race over protest, and Mike and Robin would not have been immune to the changing styles. And it might be the jokey wordplay of 'Bob Dylans 115th Dream' or the loving tongue of 'It's All Over Now Baby Blue', but young Mr Zimmerman was casting an all-embracing shadow over Britain's folk clubs. And here is that shadow on 'Dandelion Blues'. But it's a song that brings a smile, as does.

'How Happy I Am' (Heron)

This feels like Mike's companion piece. It has a happy, sing-along chorus, and lo and behold, it's all three on this track: Clive playing guitar and singing to Mike's guitar and vocal and Robin's mandolin and vocal. This was the side two opener on the original vinyl, which says a lot about the trio as a trio. As with 'Dandelion Blues', you can hear happy folkies singing along. Mike's strange vocal inflexions – sometimes hokey American, sometimes Caribbean – are to the fore here. For sure, he was listening to blues singers like Robert Johnson, but taking the blues and adding a grin: ah, there's the clever bit. That, and Robin's mandolin adding a sparkle, make this an irresistible piece of whimsy.

'Empty Pocket Blues' (Palmer)

Two trio songs in a row! As Clive's only writing credit in the ISB canon, this has maintained a great affection in ISB fandom and even within the band. Indeed, some years later, post-Clive, the band were still performing it with Licky and Rose on lead vocals. The video of this is pretty easy to find: see the last chapter on later releases for details. The song details Clive and Robin's penniless existence in Edinburgh and is indeed a blues. Perhaps the recording's most notable asset is Robin's blues whistle-playing, swooping and moaning. Standout.

Obviously, this early writing endeavour whet Clive's whistle, as his post-ISB music saw him continue to create songs, as well as build his own instruments, as we saw with the small pipes he played in the 21st century revived band. In the period of that band, I was asked to play on a solo album by Clive. I took along bombards and shawms as requested, along with some percussion and other instruments. Unfortunately, the tracks he wanted the shawm on were in a different key to that which the instrument can play in, but I played sitar and added percussion. Clive and I didn't spark it off, not helped by him being full of a heavy cold. To date, the album has not been released.

'Smoke Shovelling Song' (Williamson)
Back to Robin solo. Once again, we are in the jolly tales area. No doubt this jaunty piece set in a winter so cold that the smoke freezes solid was based on the legendary cold flat that Robin, Clive and Bert Jansch shared. The legend goes that they erected a tent in the room to provide some degree of warmth at night. It's certainly another number that smacks of writing for intimate folk club audiences. It's noticeable that the first album contains these straight-ahead 'funny' songs. Although this would hardly leave the band – through 'Big Ted', 'HiremPawnitof' and 'Waiting For You', all the way to 'Dumb Kate' – this first album holds onto the chuckles for crowd-pleasing outings.

'Can't Keep Me Here' (Heron)
Now it's Mike solo, with a pleasant little song that may refer to his longing to leave the 'prison' of his office job. Perhaps the title was a little presumptive, given the departure of both Robin and Clive after this album. Mike's writing certainly seemed more autobiographical, albeit slightly distorted. His autobiography certainly displays his yearning to get out of the nine-to-five rat race to be the troubadour he so wanted to be. Being asked to join Clive and Robin must have seemed like a gift from above, and their subsequent disappearance like having that gift snatched away. What would Mike have done if they had stayed in distant climes? We will never know. He was certainly still writing the songs that would pop up on the next album, but would the circle be broken without Robin? Speculation is all we have.

'Good As Gone' (Williamson)
Perhaps this shows a lot of things. Firstly, it shows that Robin and Mike could take a subject and approach songwriting in totally different ways. Mike couldn't be kept here; Robin was already gone. The other main standout of this track is the way there are not just tempo changes, but entire melody changes within the whole. Yes, this approach is tentative here, but it's the first pointer of the way the band would go in the future. Also, note Robin's use of runs on the lower guitar strings: a style that he made very much his own. This track just feels like a door is opening. Perhaps we read more into things when we look back. Maybe this was a precursor; it certainly felt like it. A precursor to heading south? A precursor to more intricate music? Look at 'M.1 Breakdown' on Fairport Convention's first album, for example. A silly little bluegrass-tinged

instrumental that ends in the sound of a car crashing. Within mere months, Fairport would be involved in a horrific accident on the UK's M1 motorway, killing drummer Martin Lamble and Richard Thompson's girlfriend. It's only in retrospect that these musical things resonate with significance.

'Niggertown' (Trad. Arr. Palmer)

An instrumental which, for blindingly obvious reasons, became known as 'Banjo Tune' in latter years. Clive, here solo, is on his first love: the banjo, and for the first and only time on the album. Though there are a number of spots where, in retrospect, it would have fitted in nicely: 'Smoke Shovelling Song', for example. It's a wonderful piece of old-time American banjo-playing, in a style you rarely hear anymore: lost amongst frantic Pogues-esque thrashing and blinding bluegrass picking. It may be another short instrumental, but it's so heart-lifting that it deserves its place.

'Everything's Fine Right Now' (Heron)

It may be the last track, but the trio goes out together on a perennial favourite of the band: a piece still being performed as things drew to a close in the 1970s. Mike's lyrical satisfaction – with a hint of Dylan's 'If You Gotta Go, Go Now' – is timeless. You can still sing it proudly to this day, and I betcha that people will sing along. We have Mike on guitar and vocals, Robin on mandolin and vocals, Clive on guitar, and – for the first recorded time with the ISB – the kazoo: which would be a large feature of the String Band sound, throughout.

The song continued to have a life. When Mike formed The Incredible Acoustic Band, it was one of two ISB songs that made the setlist (the other being 'Log Cabin Home In The Sky'), and it even saw primetime TV action, when a character in a TV drama about oil rig workers was depicted as an ISB fan. How many viewers knew of the band at this point is open to debate. Some probably thought they were a dramatic invention. Anyway, in a party scene, as a gift, the 'lads' book Mike and the ISB to play, and they run through the number on primetime TV.

And so, that was the first album out into the world. It served as a rather delicious soup before the main courses to follow.

The 5000 Spirits or the Layers of an Onion (1967)

Personnel:

Robin Williamson: vocals, bowed gimbri, guitar, flute, drums, rattles and mandolin

Mike Heron: vocals and guitar

with

Licorice (Christina McKechnie): vocals

Danny Thompson: string bass

Soma: sitar and tambourine

John Hopkins: piano

Joe Boyd: producer

Record label: Elektra

Release date: July 1967

Chart position: UK: 25

Running time: 50:10

As mentioned in the introduction, following that first album, both Clive and Robin took off for sunnier climes: Clive to Afghanistan and Robin (and Licorice) to Morocco. Mike was left to ply his solo trade, and Joe Boyd was left wondering if his signing would only produce the one album. Although Clive would not return to the band (at least not in the 20th century), Robin did eventually return to put the ISB back in action as a duo – most importantly for the sound: he came back with instruments from exotic places. Mostly whistles and percussion, I believe, but he also returned with a gimbri. Now, this very simple lute would be 'plucked' in normal play, but Robin – and we know not precisely why – decided to use a bow on it; A double bass bow at that. And it appeared here on this album, and a million hippies (I may be exaggerating here) went 'Wow man!'. It's haunting nasal whine was an eye-opener and perfectly fitted the Summer of Love. The whole package did. The cover was all bright colours and mystical beings. The title wasn't even on the front of the sleeve, for goodness sake. You could stare at it for hours and imagine you were tripping. To be fair, it's possible many were. On the back, an oval picture showed Mike and Robin looking stoned and godlike in dark woodland, their names in flames below, albeit the wrong way 'round (So first Robin is called Clive on a sleeve, now he's called Mike?), and above that, the title.

The title fit, what with it being the time for long titles that oozed hidden meanings: *Sgt, Pepper's Lonely Hearts Club Band*; *My People Were Fair and Had Sky in Their Hair…* – that kind of thing. I mean, the ISB were one degree of separation away from the fab four. The moptops had praised 'October Song', as had Bob Dylan, and the album cover art was by The Fool: the designers who made the brightly coloured clothes for the Apple Boutique and painted the trippy mural on the wall. The Fool even recorded a rather nice album of their own that is quite 'Stringy' in style.

But for our happy pair, this was the ground-breaker. Mike, in particular, had done the best he could as a solo performer but was not finding it easy (cf. 'Trim

Up Your Love Light' on the post-ISB Heron album, *Diamond of Dreams*, sort of tells that sad tale of falling returns). On Robin's return, Mike played him some of the new songs he had written during Robin's absence. The encounter is related in the last words of Mike's autobiography *You Know What You Could Be*. Let's talk more of that in the tracks.

My feeling is that if you want to play an album by the band to initiate a newcomer to the land of String, this is possibly the one. It's not as basic as the first album, not as off-putting as subsequent releases may be to the untrained ear. It summed up so much of the Summer of Love. To an extent, that slight sidestep allowed keener observation. Just as The Band could produce perfect American songs as a Canadian group (apart from one), or Richard Thompson could write songs of perfect Englishness as a Scot, so too could Mike and Robin write perfect English psychedelia. Yes, in a folk way – none of your Syd Barrett Stratocastering – but the rural peace through a multi-coloured filter fit perfectly.

5000 Spirits' place was marked in time in the film *The Boat That Rocked*, when the hippie DJ on the pirate-radio ship nearly drowns, rescuing it as the ship sinks, allowing lesser albums to enter Davy Jones' locker. There is light and shade. If one song seems complicated, one is simpler; if Mike's voice seems deep and warm, Licky's seems high and crystal beautiful. And the sounds of India infused the music. Light a candle, crash on a velvet beanbag, put your wine on the small Indian table, and close your eyes. The ISB have entered the building of your head, Maaaan.

'Chinese White' (Heron)

Ah, a gentle acoustic guitar riff opens up, and then, then the droning sawing whine, as the gimbri comes in. In his book, Mike refers to hearing this and realising it was special: this was the transformation for the band, the sound that lifted them above the rest, the USP in modern terms.

The title comes from the name of the white in watercolour paintboxes and, groovily, doesn't appear in the lyrics. In fact, the lyrics are dreamy: only Mike would know exactly what he was saying. But it just feels right; it just slides into the zeitgeist of the time, seeing the world through altered dreamlike perceptions. And the chorus: it mentions Christmas trees – magic ones to boot. And the time signature changes, almost a different tune too. This was the ISB growing into their own boots.

The mention of Christmas trees is interesting, as in no other respect is this a Christmas song. And yet, I still know of people who sing it at Christmas. One band even put it out at Christmas under the title 'Magic Christmas Tree'. I hope Mike got the PRS royalties.

The leap from the first album to this is profound. It's akin to the short space between The Beatles' *Rubber Soul* and *Sgt. Pepper*. The ISB had changed from a folk club band to a world music hippie band. Fasten your seat belts.

'No Sleep Blues' (Williamson)

With Danny Thompson slapping the double bass, Robin's tribute (?) to insomnia is the perfect follow-on from 'Chinese White'. It's witty rather than funny and is driven nicely along by Robin's acoustic guitar, Mike playing lead and the flute underpinning and soaring around the vocals. There is just something more assured than the first album's compositions, almost as if to say, 'Can I write songs? Yes, I can. So, off we go then'. It says everything you want it to say: apologies for waking others; scampering mice sounding louder than they are; dawn suddenly appearing. Here was the continuation of humour, but now more subtle, more knowing – almost a jump from mother-in-law jokes to observational comedy. Because everyone (even me) has suffered lack of sleep. And Robin caught that mood perfectly. Sublime.

'Painting Box' (Heron)

This was a single, though it didn't really trouble the 'hit parade'. I did see them on TV, though, on the Julie Felix programme, with the late Ms. Felix singing along, taking the part Licorice sings here – you'll find it online. Julie (who always used to send me a Christmas card) says that musicians don't often see each other because they are all on the road in different places. So it's 'groovy' to be with Mike and Robin. All the time, they sit in the background with otherworldly fixed grins. And Mike's guitar is around his neck, so let's just mention the elephant in the room right now. Assuming that you're right-handed, your guitar strap goes from the neck of the instrument, over your left shoulder, behind your neck, and your right arm is above it as it reconnects to the body of the guitar. Mike has his strap simply behind his neck, both ends in front. Why? He's the only well-known musician I've ever seen do that. I asked Rose if she knew why. She didn't. Someday I'll ask Mr. Heron himself, but until then, find the Julie Felix clip and wonder.

'Painting Box' is catchy, and in a parallel world, actually might have been a hit. In some ways, the lyrics align with 'Chinese White' – the feeling of the observations as you walk around stoned – but with a chorus that draws you into the world where fresh-faced hippie girls melted your heart. As mentioned, this is the first credited appearance of the wonderful Licorice. Her crystal-clear high vocals would become as much a part of the ISB sound as the sitar, and she makes her instrumental debut, too, with the gentle ring of the finger cymbals. Danny Thompson continues on bass duties. Those new ears should find this acceptable, I think.

'The Mad Hatter's Song' (Williamson)

And we are there. In the heart of Stringdom. Indian influences, meandering mystical lyrics, changes of tempo and melody line: one minute all raga, the next, all barrelhouse blues. And 5:40: I mean, that's at least twice the length of pop songs of the time! There is no Mike here, but Robin sings and plays his trademark bass runs on the acoustic, again, playing as you would an oud (it's pronounced ood, as in wood, by the way). John Hopkins plays piano and

Soma plays sitar and tanpura (Soma was actually Nazir Jairazbhoy) and Danny continues on the bass. For the uninitiated, this may not be the best entry – it's hard work at first. When I first heard it, I couldn't make head nor tail, but I persevered. It's worth it. There is a later album called *The Chelsea Sessions 1967* – studio outtakes from the early *5000 Spirits* sessions – which shows that Robin was quite into *Alice in Wonderland* at the time, with a companion piece called 'Alice Is A Long Time Gone'. More on that album in the final chapter on the best of the post-1974 releases.

Alice in Wonderland was, of course, a hippie favourite. The eating and drinking causing altered states, and the talking animals, were all well in line with hippiedom, not to mention the minor obsession with Victoriana, of the period: a time when you would cut quite a dash nipping down the shops dressed as a Bow Street Runner. It's fascinating that Mike is not playing sitar at this point, given his playing on the next album. Like many instruments, it's simple to play but difficult to play well. Mike took the difficult path. And won.

'Little Cloud' (Heron)

And we are into two Heron things. The jolly sweet little song with sing-along potential and the slightly calypso-tinged vocal styling. By itself, it's a slight little song, but in the context of the entire album, it works perfectly. Mike drives along on guitar with Robin going ape on drums and rattles. Both sing, and there is also an uncredited Licorice, though I'm open to correction on who the female voice is. Again, the gentle humour. Mike's calypso voice is interesting. Calypso had become a mainstream thing in Britain, following along with the Windrush generation. Its style foreshadowed rap, in that words would be improvised over the tune, and as its popularity grew, even the likes of Lance Percival – white comedy actor and part of the satire boom – would appear on TV in the evening singing a topical calypso on current affairs. In a Caribbean accent. I know. Even Bernard Cribbins made the charts with 'Gossip Calypso', so perhaps Mike just soaked it all up.

'The Eyes Of Fate' (Williamson)

More dipping into the heady mix of philosophy, religion and mysticism, which marked much of Robin's work; more flitting between melodies and an entrancing chant in 'Ory, ory…'; Mike and Robin and Licorice – Robin swapping into yet another melody near the end. It was clear that by this point, Robin had been much-influenced by the music he had experienced in North Africa. His guitar-playing had developed serious influences from the oud – the region's lute-like instrument which Robin also brought back – and indeed plays later in the album. This influence is perhaps why the ISB sound of two acoustic guitars, can sound so exotic. The ISB's style interplay is something which cannot be overlooked. Mike's powerful strum is always spot-on, and is often in a style unique to himself. Robin's guitar work is exemplary, but along with the oud, it's not difficult to hear him playing mandolin-style lines. His use of vibrato on a note is pure mandolin: there to sustain a note, as the instrument's short, small body, quickly allows notes to decay. It's not required on a larger-bodied guitar, so when Robin does it, the effect is stunning.

'Blues For The Muse' (Williamson)

Much more in standard song mode, Robin plays da' blues with aplomb. It's a good opener for side two, with Mike sucking some rather good blues harmonica. It perverts blues cliches in a very subtle way but is rather overshadowed by much of the rest of the album.

'The Hedgehog's Song' (Heron)

Mike gets out the bottleneck for another of his songs featuring bizarre third parties: hedgehogs, clouds, trees etc. It's worth comparing the song to the last album's 'Maybe Someday', in that it covers the same subject of a young man seeking love, but here things have moved on from actuality to allegory. The hedgehog is the doubt in our minds about doing the right things. It's a fantastic little song in a very quiet way. Once again, Robin's African journey adds to his rattling drums. It's easy to pass off his percussion as just a little tapping to carry the beat, but he often goes around the beat and drives along: think Keith Moon limited to a tabour and a maraca. On stage, Robin would sit behind a makeshift drum kit made up of more ethnic drums than your standard setup and play a small storm. In the *Be Glad* film, he's captured flitting from percussion to percussion, lifting the song up high.

'First Girl I Loved' (Williamson)

If you had to make a list of the most realised, the most clearly-perceived vision, this would have to be in the top three. It holds up to this day, it doesn't date, and we can probably all relate to the concept of wondering what happened to the young love that we left behind. It might be slight, but there's a real depth in the lyrics: the yearning regret at parting to pursue the life of the musician, and the line that many of us must have experienced, about never having slept together but 'making love' a thousand times. Instantly the vision of the parties with the bedroom door wedged shut on a blanket of coats. Just me? Well, fill in your own blanks on that one. Again it's a Mike-free track, though reliable Danny holds it down on bass, against Robin's guitar lines: clever without being flash. Perfect, in other words. It garnered cover versions by the likes of Judy Collins (also on Elektra), though the girl became a boy in her version, obviously. It's a sign of the song's strength that the lyrics still seem perfect for a woman to sing. Perhaps the delicacy of touch in the writing, makes this a shoe-in. Whatever – album two and already a perfect classic.

'You Know What You Could Be' (Heron)

Robin on oud, mandolin, drums, flute and vocals, leads the way to increasing use of studio overdubbing to achieve the song's sound without getting in session players. Mike's song of hope begins with a very world music, ethnic introduction, seemingly unrelated to what follows (though 'the opposite is also true'). Did Mike write in the ethnic interludes, or did Robin suggest them? It doesn't matter in the end because the ISB was now operating as a band.

The song is inspirational and is possibly an observation of Mike's earlier-life fellow office workers, worrying all the time about what they 'should be'. It's both sad and mad that the attitude endures in society today: so many doing what fits in with what other people think and not exploring their own potential.

The song provided the title for Mike's autobiography. Well worth a read, it takes his life up to the first preparations for this album and gives insight from the inside. At the time of this writing, a second volume is in preparation. In passing, the book is half Mike's story and half Andrew Greig's story: an admirer of the band, who forms his own musical ensemble in the band's image, travelling to London to try to make it, and spending time at Joe Boyd's Witchseason office. Again, at the time of this writing, Rose is preparing to write a book about Witchseason. That should be an excellent read.

'My Name Is Death' (Williamson)
Robin solo again. Although credited to Robin, this is essentially the traditional song, 'Death And The Lady', with extra words and the odd tweak here and there. Like the first album instrumentals, I've always seen this as an interlude, the moment where the roller coaster rattles on the high flat rail, before plunging inexorably down the slope to the finish.

The use of a traditional folk song as the basis for a new song is something that permeates the ISB work. 'Black Jack Davy/David' follows 'The Raggle Taggle Gypsy' song; 'Iron Stone' uses an Irish lament, and so on. More on that as the appropriate songs appear.

'Gently Tender' (Heron)
Lovely. Just lovely. Robin's flute here and throughout, ripples over the song, adding just the right level of colour to another of Mike's delight-in-the-world songs. Mike plays guitar, and – in addition to the flute – Robin contributes the only appearance of the bass gimbri, and more drums, while Licorice sings. Although Robin and Mike's writings have always been distinctively different, you could always feel they listened to and learned from each other. Mike employs voices on a quite manic second melody section, showing that, against the odds, the two voices were the perfect foil for each other, with Licorice providing the icing on the cake.

'Way Back In The 1960s' (Williamson)
And off with a smile. Robin's imagining of his old self looking back on his current self was both witty and perceptive. On the back of a bluesy tune, it's fun to realise that whatever the age, young people will always discover their

own language and way of speaking and consider what went before to be insane and ridiculous. Of course, Robin never did make his first million as such, and to this day, he does gigs too. And he almost certainly doesn't eat bacon, but it was a lovely way to close the album that would point the way to greater things for the band.

Conclusion

It's rare to find an album with no weak tracks, but the ISB managed it with *5000 Spirits*. As is often the case in a band with two writers, there tends to be a spark of friendly rivalry that ups the ante. And that seems to be the case here.

The Hangman's Beautiful Daughter (1968)

Personnel:
Robin Williamson: Vocals, guitar, gimbri, whistle, percussion, pan pipes, piano, oud, mandolin, jaws harp, chahanai, water harp, harmonica
Mike Heron: Vocals, sitar, organ, guitar, hammer dulcimer, harpsichord
With
Dolly Collins: Flute organ and piano
Licorice: Vocals and finger cymbals
Richard Thompson and Judy Dyble: Vocals on 'The Minotaur's Song'
Joe Boyd: Producer
Record label: Elektra
Release date: March 1968
Chart position: UK: 5, US: 161
Running time: 49:51

If *5000 Spirits* may be considered as the album of drifting smoke rings, then we must take *Hangman's* as the album of chemically-induced states. Gone were the sweet little songs. In their place were songs which seemed to explore the darker side of childhood. Suddenly all musical genres were fair game – if it was what was needed, that was what would be used.

Mike was no longer just the guitarist: now he was the main keyboard player and, perhaps more importantly, he had become the sitar player. From The Beatles' 'Norwegian Wood' onwards, pop had embraced this classical Indian instrument. George Harrison led the way, but even The Hollies were using it. Mike's sitar playing is much underrated, with a fluidity and perception of the instrument's potential that many others didn't quite get, usually. This was probably due to a number of factors. While many of the pop guys had done little more than use the sitar to play electric guitar lines, Mike had listened extensively to world music, including Ravi Shankar, so he was more versed in what the instrument did best. Maybe Robin's songs took him where the instrument could do no more than follow the path that was laid out. Whatever, here's to Mike Heron and his playing.

Robin was equally expanding his already extensive instrumental abilities. It's worth noting that the instrument he had been best known for in the early days – the fiddle – is totally absent on this album, while more esoteric brethren like the gimbri, take over.

Both writers' songs here were denser and more worked. In particular, Robin was going off on his own path, and Mike was certainly not too far behind.

The cover featured a wintry shot of the duo, outlined against the blue sky, snow clinging to the drystone wall: Mike in a brown, woollen 'thing', Robin in sweeping black cloak topped by a black wide-brimmed hat. They stare at the camera with eyes that seemed to see beyond you. On the rear of the sleeve, the hippie commune is gathered in the woods: men, women and children, all of whom appeared to my eyes to have raided the dressing-up box. Robin holds a rattle (?), his expression giving you the impression that this relic is a holy imparter of wisdom. Mike holds a homemade mask made by a child, the sort of things parents pin to their kitchen walls. To the front-right, Licorice holds Leaf the dog: her long dark hair framing a face that every boy felt was the ideal of the hippie chick they would surely meet one day. A little behind, fresh from Yorkshire, Rose Simpson makes her first appearance on an ISB sleeve, ducking under a branch.

In later issues, the sleeve would be flipped so the rear would become the front: an ISB tradition where sleeves would be available in different configurations, which we had already seen with the first album's UK/US sleeves. In some respects, it's a difficult album, though the 'heads' of 1968 would have felt that that was just how it should be. It's strange then that this marked the high point of their chart success.

The album title can be explained in a few ways. Mike has said that it refers to the hangman being death, and the beautiful daughter, the afterlife; and also that the hangman is the first years of their lives, and the beautiful daughter is their life now (or then, now, well, you know what I mean). Robin said the hangman was the Second World War, and the beautiful daughter was the post-war generation and their flower power ideals. In any case, the reader can decide on the image they like best because it's an iconic title.

If we take the received wisdom that the major ISB albums are numbers two to four, then it's possible to ascribe seasons to them. *5000 Spirits* is spring: fresh and naive, but full of promise; *Wee Tam and the Big Huge* is summer into autumn: the warmth relaxing into mellow fruitfulness, the days growing shorter. But *Hangman's* is Winter. It may be cold, but we can huddle in front of the roaring fire and tell our stories, remember our childhoods, the good and the bad, and scare each other with ghost stories.

Returning to our new ears, I would suggest that this is not the entry-level album. 'A Very Cellular Song' may be one of ISB's better-known works, but to the modern ear, ten minutes is a long time. That said, this is a phenomenal achievement: a moment in time that encapsulates the hippie movement, in the years before harder drugs made haggard the face of the beautiful daughter.

'Koeeoaddi There' (Williamson)

As I mentioned, this is a difficult album for the casual listener. So it's a mark of that, that the opening track is one of the easier pieces. The title, purportedly, comes from Robin pulling out Scrabble tiles at random and making a word from what appeared. How you pronounce it is anybody's guess. Do you take the two d's as a 'th', such as you would in Welsh? No matter, it's a charming song about Robin's childhood. Or not. Robin has often blurred his past, sometimes making it fit into a reality. (cf. 'Mad Girl' from Robin's later solo work, which purports to explain the slight scar on his face but is a fiction.)

The telltale sign here is the mention of Licorice, who, as far as we know, Robin didn't meet in his childhood. The reality is that it's probably a rich mix of his real past and fictional embellishments.

This song shows more exploration of the lots-of-songs-tied-together approach, starting on a steadily-strummed drone, passing through a slow waltz and faster sections. But as an opener, it does lay things before you. Mike's now the go-to sitar man: an instrument learned to offer a foil to Robin's multi-instrumental skills. And yet, even in this simple song, the ISB trademarks are there: opening on a single simply-strummed chord and almost-chanted vocals before a guitar filigree takes us to 3/4 waltz time and Happy Valley pond. Incidentally, that is a real place and still exists to this day. After that, we are into a child's riddle against a skipping-rope type of tune. Robin also takes his voice way down low here, displaying his huge vocal range, which also exists even to this day.

'The Minotaur's Song' (Williamson)

Eclectic or what? Though still thought of as a folk band, ISB were working their way into creating their own space, and going straight into a homage to Gilbert and Sullivan was definitely taking things in a unique direction for a 'folk band'. 'The Minotaur's Son' featured a mass chorus of Mike, Licorice, Rose Simpson, Judy Dyble (ex Fairport) and Richard Thompson (still Fairport at this stage). To be honest, you could insert this into a G&S operetta, and most people wouldn't notice the join. Mike's piano, the groans and noises from the singers, the clapping and faux Chinese talk, all combine to delight.

It fits, of course, with the interest in all things Victorian at that time: in clothes and in style (if not with the urban planners who were pulling down Victorian buildings at a pace). Couple it with the ancient myths of the Minotaur, and there is a winning combination for the time. The Minotaur myth still remains strong, even appearing in *Doctor Who* twice (under the name of the Nimon, with both Tom Baker and Matt Smith).

'Witches Hat' (Williamson)

Mike on hammer dulcimer, Robin on guitar and whistle. A neglected little hippie gem. On a personal note, in the early 1970s, I sat in Bradford city centre at eight in the morning singing this. My companion on backing vocals was called Rob. Rob liked the ISB and played keyboards in prog rock bands. His hair was long, straight and blonde, and he resembled a young Rick Wakeman. We always called him Rockstar. I wonder where he is now?

Like many of Robin's lyrics, you can make your own mind up as to what they mean, but it swings from gentle minor chords to rhythmic la-la-la's. The opening guitar part makes use of the D minor chord fingering. 'Sitting on his head like a paraffin stove' always brings to mind the line from Douglas Adams' *The Hitchhiker's Guide to the Galaxy*, which says, 'It hung in the air in exactly the way that a brick doesn't'.

'A Very Cellular Song' (Heron)

So then, if you were wondering why Robin was grabbing all the credits thus far, here is the reason: Mike's thirteen-minute opus purportedly detailing an LSD trip. It marks Mike fully embracing the use of multiple sections within one song. Mike's keyboards largely tie the song together, harpsichord and organ repeating an unusual but mesmerising chord sequence. Robin adds colour in perfect style: a whistle here, percussion there, vocals here, gimbri there. And Licorice speaks a line that anyone who hears never forgets: 'Amoebas are very small'. Certainly, Nigel Planer never did: he incorporated that section of the song into his album made under his *The Young Ones* guise of Neil, the hippie.

The song opens with the basic chord progression underpinning the piece before breaking off into a section taken from The Carter Family repertoire, under the title of 'Goodnight'. Not for the only time in ISB, there is Christian imagery within the lyrics. The basic sequence returns before the amoebas enter for a gentle organ-based section, the whole thing ending on a joyous repeated chorus of 'May the long time sun shine on you'. A perfect end, a perfect sentiment for the time. Of course, at the height of the new wave hippy rejection, this was all the ammo the detractors needed to point to the airy-fairy flower child ramblings. But in truth, this was a radical statement, even for its time. Thankfully, in a few more years, a reassessment took place, and the ISB CD re-releases became the best-selling reissues on Elektra. Such is the rolling view of history.

Lyrically, it strides from one idea to the next: crystalised ginger is stolen; people ride backwards on giraffes; amoebas just give a wriggle. It certainly displays the essence of a good trip (even if, like myself, you've only experienced such things second-hand). And while Paul McCartney was rounded on for admitting to taking LSD, this piece was largely ignored by 'the straights', no doubt because the ISB were thought to play for the ones who were there anyway, and not the teenage girls who might drop a tab because Pauly says it's cool.

Another of the early repertoire that reappeared in the 21st-century reformation.

'Mercy I Cry City' (Heron)

Mike opens side two of the vinyl with a 'let's get our heads together in the country, man' song of the dirt and grime of the city. Man, does Straightsville bring you down. Bummer. The concert footage in the *Be Glad for the Song Has No Ending* film shows Robin playing harmonica and whistle, swapping from one to the other rapidly, and tapping percussion too. Whether he did this in the studio is open to debate, but its jaunty style prevents it from becoming a mawkish harangue – perhaps a companion to Joni Mitchell's 'Big Yellow Taxi'. In the end – for all its putting-down of urban living – the whole thing is turned on its head when Robin utters the line, 'The opposite is also true'.

Later, post-ISB, Mike would sing in his song, 'Residential Boy', that they were 'just a couple of city boys/We couldn't even sing the blues', and that they were 'raised on street lights', so maybe he felt the need to debunk the ISB's pastoral aura.

'Waltz Of The New Moon' (Williamson)

The first of two 'difficult' Robin songs on side two. Let's face it, few bands would start a song with the line, 'I hear the Emperor of China used to wear iron shoes with ease'. The lyrics continue to mix philosophies from various points, with the beauty of nature and who knows what else. For many, this was the attraction. There was a striving in this period for reaching out and exploring the inner self, sparked by The Beatles, the Maharishi and the use of psychedelic drugs. Robin had hit the motherlode. The a cappella group, Baccapella, formed (as Sharon and the Students, from misheard Macedonian, and because nobody was called Sharon or was a student) by the late Peter Bellamy, were thinking of covering this. It's a shame they didn't, as it would have been awesome in the true sense of the word.

'The Water Song' (Williamson)

And here was Dolly Collins on her medieval flute organ. She and sister Shirley had been dabbling in fusing early music with folk music, culminating in the groundbreaking *Anthems in Eden*. Robin had even contributed a song to it: 'God Dog'. It was not recorded by the ISB, though it did appear on the *The Chelsea Sessions 1967* album as a demo. Shirley and Dolly Collins were undoubtedly fellow travellers, though their Sussex upbringing had led them into traditional music rather than composing. Having said that, Dolly's arrangements were very close to the original composition. Sadly, Dolly passed away some years back, but Shirley is still with us and is lauded as one of the true greats of English folk music.

The musical collaboration here brings forth untold beauty and simplicity, a wonderful lull from the intensity of 'Waltz Of The New Moon'. The sound of Robin splashing water in a bowl and of natural waterfalls (and that's pretty much the instrumental break) allows the listener to drift into contentment. Its strength as a song can be gauged by it being one of the few Robin songs performed during the 21st century Mike-and-Clive version of the ISB, with Fluff and Dando as a duo. See the last chapter for more on that.

'Three Is A Green Crown' (Williamson)

When I was a callow youth, not yet twenty, I worked on computers, changing tapes and discs, and generally being modern. On the night shift, the computers would simply process data, so there was little call for us operators to do much except keep an eye on things. Consequent to that, we worked on an hour-on-hour-off basis at night, and in our hours off, we had a portable record deck and would play our albums. Playing *Hangman's* would see me roundly berated and even threatened with violence if I didn't take it off! And this was the song that would break the camel's back. Based largely around the sitar in strong raga mode with occasional diversions into other snatches of melody, the just-short-of-eight-minute piece was more than enough for my fellow technocrats.

In truth, it was hard-going for me too, but it repays your attention with such snatches of beauty that perseverance is rewarded – as much of the music of this period did. To this day, I find that if I instantly love some piece of music, I probably will always hold an affection for it. But if I hear something that makes no sense, but sparks something that makes me want to understand, then my passion will remain forever. Yes, as my own musical skills have developed, I can more readily decipher, but 'Three Is A Green Crown' continues to reveal itself in new ways. I remember seeing John Martyn on *The Old Grey Whistle Test* and being perplexed by the mumbling drawl. But I persevered. John in the real world could be a total arsehole, but the art, not the artist, keeps me enthralled. Mike and Robin and Rose and Malcolm have always been lovely.

'Swift As The Wind' (Heron)
This song disturbed me then and still does now. Mike's song evokes the terrors of childhood so graphically, that you can feel the horror you once felt as the branch tapped at your bedroom window, that was for sure the bony fingers of a witch come for you – that creak on the staircase was a wolfman who had dispatched your parents and was now coming for you. Robin's wailing backing vocals simply heighten the feeling Mike's chugging minor chords bring on. There's blood and swords; there's chariots and wings. And as the pace drops and your parents soothe you, there are strange bangs and clatters, and you wonder if they have been replaced by androids! It's an amazing song, a million miles from pretty clouds and helpful hedgehogs.

Post-ISB, fans produced a couple of albums performing ISB numbers: *The Hangman's Beautiful Granddaughter* and *Winged We Were*. For the latter, I chose this song for my contribution. I was even scared singing and playing it. If *The Hangman's Beautiful Daughter* was winter, here was the coldest day of the season.

'Nightfall' (Williamson)
So after all that, time to be soothed by a gentle, lilting Robin song. The sitar perfectly counterpoints his soaring, swooping voice. Listening to the album in bed at night (You didn't have a record deck in your bedroom??), it was perfect. The disturbing men with swords, the choking tubes, the Minotaurs, the Emperors in iron shoes, all melted away, leaving only the 33 1/3 click of the needle on the playoff track. Goodnight, beautiful daughter.

Conclusion
So there is the album that has become a legend. An album that made you wonder just where their heads were at to create such stuff. Approach with caution, but when the dog wags its tail and licks your hand, you will be hooked forever.

Wee Tam and The Big Huge (1968)

Personnel:
Robin Williamson: vocals, guitar, bass, gimbri, percussion, sarangai, violin, harpsichord, piano, organ, flute, kazoo, harmonica, Celtic harp, drums
Mike Heron: vocals, guitar, bass, harpsichord, washboard, percussion, harmonica
With
Rose Simpson: Violin, percussion, backing vocals
Licorice McKechnie: vocals, percussion, Celtic harp
Joe Boyd: Producer
Record label: Elektra
Release date: November 1968
Chart position: US: 174 (Wee Tam), US: 180 (The Big Huge)
Running time: 86:48

The boys were big. They'd hit the spot at just the right time, and listening to what else was around; they'd done it on their own terms. They could play in America, but many better-known bands struggled. Somehow, two eclectic acoustic musicians had made it in a world of drums and increasingly loud electrics, which was cool. Because some bands reach this point and lose their heads, think they're the bee's knees and lose it by album four, until they get scared enough to pull themselves together. But not here. In the same year that had seen the release of *Hangman's*, they had gotten together just shy of 90 minutes worth of new material: enough for a double album. A double album without filler. It's hard to envisage *Wee Tam and the Big Huge* edited down to a single album, as perhaps you could, arguably, with The Beatles' *White Album*. WTATBH had depth and breadth. The two songwriters had differing styles, but those styles complemented each other and balanced the album. It managed to be varied and cohesive at the same time. Many will tell you that this is the final classic album the band made; that after this, it was all downhill. Well, I'd disagree, but if you subscribe to that other view, then this is a hell of a way to go out. There is experimentation in styles and genres, but it never goes too far.

And behold the full crediting of Rose and Licorice. More was afoot in that direction, but leave that for another horse, later.

So, let's start with the cover. As originally issued on vinyl, you were confronted with the lyrics, who plays what, and the titles, all in gentle script with fancy illumination for the first letter of each song. 'Look', it seemed to say, 'this is serious stuff. Forget us posing on an old bus or the like. We are the words, the words are us'. Lyrics on sleeves weren't a thing, really. *Sgt. Pepper* had kind of put it into the pop world, but this was a step further. On the inside, the duo sat beatifically smiling, all floppy hats, beads, ladies blouses and ruffles. The photographs – trivia fans – were taken in Frank Zappa's garden.

And now the question. Is this really a double album? Well, yes, that is how it was conceived and how it was issued. But Elektra were windy about the sales of an expensive item like a double, so decided to also offer it as two single albums: not Part 1 and Part 2, but individually as *Wee Tam* and *The Big Huge*. And that is really how it has remained for these many years: most reissues present the album in that way. It's too long for a single CD anyway.

Wee Tam and *The Big Huge* remains, for many fans, the quintessential ISB album. It encompasses the breadth of vision that they had been building towards. Again, for a number of fans, this was the zenith, and all was downhill from here on in, though that remains highly debatable. Compare it, if you will, to The Beatles' *Sgt. Pepper*: were their *Revolver* and the *White Album* actually better? Does it matter? After all, we're all still here...

WTATBH is an album with something for everybody. Well, almost everybody. My partner can't take the voices of Mike or Robin, under any circumstances. Takes all sorts. And yes, we are still together.

The dipping into musical styles was still under control. In later times, the band were accused of playing in a style for no other reason than they simply could. But here, the assimilation of school hymns, Woody Guthrie and old-time country just seems natural, like footnotes in a book saying, 'Hey, if you like this, you might also want to look at...'. These were the years of being 'turned on' to stuff. 'Justin came 'round last night. We smoked a couple of numbers and he turned me on to this cat called Tolkien. Man, it blew my mind.' Well, you know how it goes.

'Job's Tears' (Williamson)

'We're all still here' is the first line of the first song and as gentle an opening statement as you could wish for. With ISB having built up a reputation for exotic overdubs, it's refreshing that the album opens with just Robin's guitar, not to mention him sharing the lead vocal with Licky, rather than her on harmony on this. But it's magical. When I first heard it, I was unable to believe that what I was hearing was of this world, but that rather, a portal had opened to some mystical land. And I'd never even read *Lord of the Rings*! Well, okay, perhaps a tad pretentious, but the song is remarkable and a true showcase of Robin's range, opening with an almost crystal-perfect high, so high that when Licky comes in even higher, you wonder how long it will be before only dogs can hear them.

Like much of the ISB work of the time, the lyrics seem to carry Christian mythology. But you feel other cultures pulling so that it takes on the mantle of telling a story, rather than simply preaching. Sublime.

'Puppies' (Heron)

Lots of instrumental doubling up, here. Yes, Mike and Robin both play guitar, but, fairly inexplicably, both also play bass guitar. This is the first time the bass appeared with the ISB and the first time an electric instrument (aside from organ) had appeared too. I've tried to see who, how and why, but can't. Possibly, a part needed re-recording and the original player wasn't available. No matter, it works. Mike also contributes sitar, and Robin, gimbri and percussion.

Less lyrically complex than 'Job's Tears', it's still a lovely statement that, as great as music is, it can never match the wonder of creation and life: exemplified by the puppies wobbling around the morning kitchen or the birds outside singing without any thought of it being other than natural.

Mike's sitar-playing was perfect here, adding touches when needed without overwhelming the song. It was Mike settling into the way the duo worked as a pair to create a whole. And on this album, perhaps most of all, it works.

Although I've never performed 'Puppies', I remain entranced by the song, and have many times noodled with the opening verse: 'Even the birds when they sing, it's not everything to them'.

'Beyond The See' (Heron)
An instrumental. Long time no see. (See what I did there?) Whereas the jigs of the first album seemed to be interruptions that simply stopped the action for a pleasant interlude, here we have music that is an integral part of what is around it. Mike keyboards it up on organ and harpsichord, while Robin plays a slinky whistle and a grounding bass guitar, punctuating with a little gimbri here and there. I wonder: was it conceived as an instrumental or as a song whose lyrics didn't quite work?

'The Yellow Snake' (Williamson)
This has one verse of five lines, in which Robin paints a picture of some tropical area, with secrets never revealed. Now, that takes real skill, and Robin delivers, playing guitar and serangai (an Indian bowed instrument which varies in form between the regions. Think a sort of small bowed sitar.).
It's perfectly languorous and soporific, and even the coiling snake doesn't disturb. Is the character in the song lying there dead, like the violets he holds in his hand? It reminds me of an old oil painting that keeps revealing more as you look at it.

'Log Cabin Home In The Sky' (Heron)
Ms. Rose Simpson of Otley, Yorkshire, Mike's lover – who had sung on *The Hangman's Beautiful Daughter* – here plays violin alongside Robin. As an aside, I went to stay with Rose a few months back, and she had just resurrected the fiddle that had not been opened since the day she left the ISB. At one point during the stay, we both had our fiddles out and played this together. You can imagine the size of the tingle in my spine: the same fiddle you hear here, in a case still saying 'Incredible String Band' on it in bright green paint.

But I digress. This is the band at their most accessible. Mike drives the waltz-time slice of old-timey country along, with guitar and washboard, as the catchy chorus lifts up your heart and voice simultaneously. Debate may rage as to how much of the melody was Mike's, and how much came from traditional sources, but in the end, that's a dead-end, because it's just joyous and was a great way to wind up side one of the vinyl album.

I have a particular affection for the song. It was those 1970s students in the student's bar at Bradford University, who sang it with a guitar and a kazoo, that made me prick my ears up; made me think, 'Where is that song from?'; made me find out, buy the albums, go to the concerts; made me a Stringhead. Whoever you were, thank you.

'You Get Brighter' (Heron)

Mike's harpsichord reappears here with a pacey little number that presents a love song: to Rose, or the sun? Dunno. But aren't the best songs the ones you can interpret as you will and find they totally fit? Robin contributes guitar, and that's all there is instrumentally on the track. It's a tribute to Joe Boyd's production that this doesn't feel sparse, but like baby bear's porridge: just right.

The vocals are, of course, a major part of how ISB songs work. No vocals are credited on the album. Maybe they decided that the two voices were so uniquely distinct and that it was the writer who took lead vocals anyway. And you weren't going to mistake Licky and her voice, were you?

Things only become a little more mystical at the end, with the repeated chant of 'Krishna colours on my wall/They taught me how to love you'. So maybe it is a hymn of sorts, not a love song.

This was the other song I chose for the fan albums. I added didgeridoo and alto sax, amongst other instruments. But in the end, it was the song that shone through.

'The Half-Remarkable Question' (Williamson)

More on the mixed-mythology front, and perhaps a hint more of *Alice in Wonderland* as the chess pieces are moved by forces unseen. Maybe this piece is as near to *The Hangman's Beautiful Daughter* as anything else here, but it is far more accessible than a piece like 'Three Is A Green Crown'. It strives to answer the eternal questions of life, the universe and everything but avoids this being an imperative – more a 'just like to know' kind of thing. There is something so charmingly childlike about referring to the Earth and its 'bigness', that disarms pretension.

Again, there is the simple accompaniment of Robin's guitar and percussion, given colour by Mike's sitar. In a short-lived tribute band that played at the Leeds ISB convention, Kate Green and Raymond Greenoaken named the ensemble, The Half Remarkable Questionnaires. Neat. Incidentally, Raymond and I are also in an ISB tribute band (no dressing up, just the songs) called The Glad Undertakers. If you're going to quote, keep obscure, eh?

'Air' (Heron)

Again, debate rages as to how much of this was a traditional Hawaiian melody and how much of it is Mike. But all agree that the whole is a sing-along just made for dreamily sitting 'round the dying flames of a camp fire, singing along with your lover by your side. Just me? Oh well. Mike's organ leads, with him adding a guitar strum while Robin plays a balancing flute over the top. The lyrics are again full of wonder, regarding how something we can't see sustains everything.

I always found the line, 'I kiss your blood', mildly erotic. Just me, for sure, on that one.

'Ducks On A Pond' (Williamson)
I mentioned the childlike feel that permeates the album before, and that is perhaps no more so than here. For the first time, Robin really uses the studio, playing guitar, piano, kazoo and bass drum, while Mike adds percussion and harmonica. Again, there's a hint of Christian imagery, but the mysticism is undercut by the simple beauty of the ducks on the pond. While there are changes of key and tempo scattered around, it's never heavy-handed or extreme, and the 'sing me something' lines maintain the air of childhood wonder. In the end, it all tumbles into a children's song – 'Boys and Girls Come Out To Play' – which itself transforms into Woody Guthrie's 'Ain't Got No Home In This World Anymore'. They had used this form live, and it works here.

This was another song revived by the later ISB: post-Robin, with Clive taking the vocals and playing the banjo. A glimpse perhaps of an ISB that Clive had stuck with?

End of side two (Or end of *Wee Tam*).

'Maya' (Williamson)
I always found sides three and four to be a harder version of one and two. Thus, 'Maya' relates to 'Job's Tears' in my mind. 'Maya' puts more beautiful pictures in your head, that can mean what Robin intended, or whatsoever you decide. Mike's sitar again accompanies Robin's guitar and bass, and Rose and Licky are credited for percussion. The song is obviously a favourite of Robin's, as it has surfaced in his post-ISB solo performances in the 21st century.

The song ends abruptly on a reverberated voice, as birdsong fades up. It has transpired that Joe Boyd regrets doing this now and wishes he'd let things end differently. But for those further away from the epicentre, the birdsong is how it ends and twill ever be thus and perfect as it stands. Maya is the Mayan sun god, by the way, with many myths and legends surrounding him. So now you know. And yes, I thought Maya was a female deity too. Incidentally, why do gods have gender? There's something to ponder on.

'Greatest Friend' (Heron)
Mike is here solo (instrumentally at least) and Dylan-esque on guitar and harmonica. It's always harmonica on ISB albums: you can't call it a harp, otherwise, you could get confused with, well, a harp. And who is this guru who has given Mike all these precious gifts? Again, the ISBs across-the-board appeal

in the philosophy stakes lies with the non-specific nature of the words, and the waltz-time here is simple and compelling. It's the most Dylan-esque of all the ISB output.

'The Son of Noah's Brother' (Williamson)

I'm not sure if this is in *The Guinness Book of Records* or not, but at just 16-seconds-long, it must have been the shortest recorded song ever, until speed metal appeared anyway. It even has two instruments – Robin on guitar and Mike on organ – and the music simply descends down through the chords to just two lines. Considering its brevity, it's amazing how it sticks in your head.

'Lordly Nightshade' (Williamson)

You know those dreams you have, where everything is just madness and famous people pop up and do unfeasible things? Well, one suspects Robin had one following a rather extensive cheese-consuming session. But rather than make a cup of tea and go to work, he wrote a song about it. They are all here: Hitler, Oliver Twist, hippies, bags of coal as hats... I mean, who knows? We are again in waltz territory, and Robin sits behind the drum kit with a neat 1-2-3 underpinning. He also plays guitar, piano, and a whistle that darts around like a demented lark. Mike wisely sticks to percussion. I actually love this one, though it's perhaps one of the most overlooked tracks on the album. Robin has tended to use his dreams as source material: see, for example, 'Darling Belle', later in the book. Maybe that's where I went wrong. I forget mine as soon as I wake.

'The Mountain of God' (Williamson)

And so we reach the end of side three, with Robin on organ, and he and Mike singing their way through a medley of hymns, prayers and children's songs, after an opening line from Robin. In amongst this is 'Hark! The Herald Angels Sing', and Christopher Robin saying his prayers. It's all so nostalgic, and the lyric actually seems to bypass any preaching, simply appearing to say, 'Aren't these nice words?'. And it all ends on 'Amen'. School assembly over, please return to your classrooms.

I suspect that many of our generation have a good deal of affection for those morning assemblies in school. Our hearty little voices lifted in unison to a god many of us didn't even believe in. The song is credited to Robin, so one must assume copyright had expired on the pieces of music used.

'Cousin Caterpillar' (Heron)

Well, we had the hedgehog and the clouds, now here's the caterpillar, whose message is that things change, so just get on with it – along with the acknowledgement that most people don't. So, as Mike plays acoustic, Robin plays bass, and Rose plays percussion, we have a terrific little sing-along, complete with poppy 'doo dah' sections sung by all four band members (or all fours as will shortly be), and we go from caterpillar to butterfly, and the cousin never goes, 'Oh lord, I've lost most of my legs! It's all over!', but simply takes for granted the lovely new wings and flies off – just like most humans don't. In the ISB repertoire, it was Mike's songs that seemed to get rearranged and re-represented, as we shall see later with 'The Tree' and 'Black Jack Davy/David'. 'Cousin Caterpillar' was later given a massive rearrangement with clarinets, for the later version of the band's live gigs, but here is the real thing.

The doo-dah's are the first pop world quote that the band ever used, albeit from the already archaic 1950s doo-wop vocal groups. Nobody exists in a musical vacuum, but the ISB did their best to.

'The Iron Stone' (Williamson)

Throughout the band's tenure, Robin never totally strayed from his Celtic roots, and this simple tale of finding an unusual stone on a beach has a real Scottish/Irish feel to it, interspersed with faster sections where Mike's sitar brings the fires of India to Robins guitar backing. Rose and Licky play percussion, and the latter also plays Celtic harp, though it amounts to little more than running down the strings. But, that's the essence of ISB philosophy, as Robin once said: 'You don't have to be a virtuoso on an instrument, you just need to play enough to make the sound that you need'. And, as punctuation, Licky's run down the harp, does that in spades. This might be a good time to mention Robin's pronunciation of 'iron' as 'eye-ron'. There, I mentioned it, so let's move on. Again, there's a change of pace as the Celtic meets India in between verse interludes.

'Douglas Traherne Harding' (Heron)

There are many songs that open with a line that leaves you gaping. Mike manages that feat here with 'When I was born I had no head', and it gets no less freaky as it goes on. Much is drawn from what Mike was reading at the time. The joy of the ISB at this point was they had avoided the bandwagon-jumping. The Beatles had gone to the Maharishi, and everyone followed into the depths of Eastern religions and philosophy. Donovan was in India with The Beatles, and even the guitar-smashing Pete Townshend was into Meher Baba. Others picked up sitars and chanted. But the ISB seemed only to travel around with a philosophy shopping bag, getting two ounces of one thing, an ounce of another, and a quarter of something else. Then they would mix it all up. 'Douglas Traherne Harding' was a song that exemplified this idea to me. Yes, you can look up the details of what the lyrics are channelling (easier now we have the internet), but it's still a beautifully put together little song. Mike's a great rhythm guitarist, chugging things along using the mid to low tones (though why he wears his strap like that, nobody but him knows), and here he does just that, as Robin's fiddle flits around like a bee in a rose garden, accompanied by his percussion and whistle. Mike continues to perform the song to the present day.

'The Circle Is Unbroken' (Williamson)

If 'Iron Stone' was hinting at Celtic heritage, here Robin moves one step further, hinting at what will come in his post-ISB career. The melody is actually an Irish tune that Robin adapted, and the words align to the yearning lyrics of many an Irish lament. The underpinning here is Mike's organ, providing a soft drone beneath the vocals. Robin merely punctuates with whistle and Celtic harp: the instrument which may be classed as his post-ISB mainstay. Lyrically, there is the sound of a being standing outside the passage of time, watching and waiting 'beyond the years', ready to encourage what comes next. No matter how worldly the ISB were, they were always Scottish.

What came next, we shall see in the next chapter, as two become four, officially, as they climb off the horse they were on, to mount another steed.

Conclusion

For myself and many others, *Wee Tam and the Big Huge* was the crowning achievement. This is not to denigrate what followed, just to mark the wonder and joy this double album still brings to my heart.

Changing Horses (1969)

Personnel:
Robin Williamson: vocals, piano, washboard, flute, sarangai, Chinese banjo, percussion, electric guitar, acoustic guitar, organ, gimbri, violin
Mike Heron: vocals, electric guitar, piano, acoustic guitar, vibraphone, percussion, sitar, mandolin
Licorice McKechnie: Vocals, acoustic guitar, organ, kazoo, percussion
Rose Simpson: vocals, bass guitar, percussion
With
Walter Grundy: harmonica
Ivan Pawle: piano and organ
Joe Boyd: producer
Record label: Elektra
Release date: November 1969
Chart position: UK: 30, US: 166
Running time: 50:03

Changing horses? It is received wisdom that this was the beginning of a downward slide, and though it may not live up to the intense burst of creativity and invention which hallmarked its three predecessors, it is by no means the disaster many would have you believe. Nor is it a stutter in the creative endeavour to expand the scope and aural textures.

The album title *Changing Horses* is said to refer to the abandonment of the drug culture to embrace Scientology. Like all bands of the time, they were searching for the inner light to guide them on, and if not an Indian guru, then why not a religion that was supposed to enhance all your being? Well, here is not the place to debate the rights and wrongs of Scientology, although all ISB members have now left the organisation and seem to consider their joining as a bit of a mistake. Did it influence the music? – which is, of course, why we are here: well, probably. All life decisions do change a writer's perspective, but it would be some time before it became truly noticeable.

But there were many changes at this period as the swinging sixties became the orange and brown seventies. Firstly, and most obviously, the two women were now officially band members, not just occasional stage and studio visitors. The legend goes that Robin decided that Licky should join the band. So, not wishing to be outnumbered, Mike went home and thrust a bass guitar into Rose's hands, saying, 'Here, learn this, your in the band'. Well, that's the legend, and I refer you to Rose's autobiography for the full eye witness story. But there they were on the cover, in some ways looking reflective of the slight differences between the two pairs. They all sit on a low tree, somewhere green: a park in the USA in fact. Robin looks left, his arm outstretched with long hair falling over his shoulder, draped in something white and flimsy. He looks like nothing but some god, dropped into this universe to guide us. He sports a droopy 'tache too, for heaven's sake. Near him, looking towards, but through, the camera, is Licky. Her feet are bare, she has a band of flowers in her dark brown hair and wears a long deep-red crushed-velvet dress with pinkish puffed sleeves at the top of the arms. In short, she is the perfect hippy chick that us mere lads never seemed to meet. Below them is Mike, more grounded, with silken loon pants and a blouse-style shirt, all stripes with a ruffle at the front. He smiles broadly. I'm not sure Mike has any other expression. And on the floor is Rose, looking very gipsy-girl with an embroidered white cotton blouse and a long pale blue skirt. She smiles happily as Mike strokes her neck. Well, okay, says the ISB fan of the time, nothing too drastic going on here.

But instrumentally, things 'were' a little different. A quick scan of the back sleeve showed mucho bass action, courtesy of Rose, and the electric guitar was suddenly present. Whether this was simply because the growing circumstances of the band allowed this – where, before, it would have been impractical – or whether they were looking to be more 'commercial', I cant say. But the playing is restrained and locked into lead lines rather than thrashed chords. But there was still the grab-bag of exotic ethnicity, so let's move on. Nobody shouted 'Judas!', to my knowledge.

Let's mention that the band played Woodstock around this period. Legend relates that much went wrong, and again I refer you to Rose's account of events. Suffice to say; it was many years before any of the ISB Woodstock performance appeared on film, on record or anything. That's probably all we need to know here.

But let us return to the subject of the band expanding to a four-piece. Many, as I say, took the introduction of the girls as the beginning of the end. They weren't musicians in the way Mike and Robin were. And yet, both Rose and Licky had contributed excellent work to the albums of the ascendancy: Licky with vocals neither heard before or since. They were vocals that marked the band out. In Licky, they had a member who could do what neither of the core duo could do musically. She sang in a high female voice. And wasn't 'A Very Cellular Song' enhanced by her spine-tingling spoken line? Don't we all remember it? If the band had brought in an outside female voice, it wouldn't have worked a fraction as well – on top of which, she was competent on a few instruments, so would fill out the sound. Equally, Rose had been heard since *Hangman's*, with a naive but attractive voice, and further played the fiddle with much aplomb. I have always found the fiddle to be an instrument that enhances your playing of other instruments. Its fretless neck means the player must develop a good ear so that they know when they are just out of pitch on a note, without a fret to make it accurate for them. And accuracy is something else; your finger must go to the spot without a guide. So, from the off, despite the legend, Rose was a beautiful bass player. Rose has told me she doesn't consider herself a musician – just someone who can be told where to put her fingers and follow those instructions. I disagree to an extent. While her mind may be primarily playing on her chickens and whatever, it still doesn't change the fact that she doesn't feel stiff in her playing.

Overall, my feeling is that anyone can play music if, A: They really want to, and B: People don't tell them that they can't. When I told my school teachers that I would like to be a musician, they smirked and said I better start practising scales, pass my O level and A level, and get into a conservatoire for some years before I could even think about. I nearly stopped. But then four lads with northern accents not too far from my own, popped up, and I got a guitar and ignored my teachers. But not everybody can do that. Unknowingly, Rose and Licky became icons and inspired other women to stand on a stage and be part of a band – not just the chick with the beehive hair, singing, while the boys did the proper stuff. In her autobiography, *Boys, Clothes, Music*, Viv Albertine of the anarcho-punk all-female group, The Slits, names Rose and Licky as inspirations that made her pick up a guitar. The ripples spread far.

'Big Ted' (Williamson)

At first glance, this jolly little song about a (real) pig seemed to be standard ISB fare – another beast to add to the menagerie. But hark! Is that not a twangy electric guitar entering so early in the song? And twangy it is, merely offering a little twiddle here and there – I mean, heavy rock it ain't, but it was a new sound, and probably one which would now fit right in, as Rose's bass underpinned the music from here on in. The bass – one assumes the one present here – was a Hofner violin-style bass, made famous by one Paul McCartney. Rose played with a style and grace which went beyond her newfound acquaintance with the instrument. She says she was just shown what to play and followed those instructions with little idea of what she was doing. As an occasional bass player myself, I beg to differ. Well, okay, perhaps she didn't know what she was doing technically, but you don't get a feel like that unless you feel the music in you. Incidentally, according to Dave Pegg of Fairport Convention, the Hofner bass was his, which he lent to the band and never saw again. Rose has no recollection of this being the case, nor where it went, though she thinks it's possible that Stevie Winwood bought it. Whatever, in subsequent years, live photos and videos show the instrument played by the band to be a red Gibson SG bass. One for the instrument nerds there.

Anyway, back to 'Big Ted', where both Mike and Robin play piano – again, you can't see the join – and Walter Gundy plays harmonica. The occasional guests who appeared on the albums are interesting. Dolly Collins' flute organ, and Danny Thompson's string bass, both provided instrumentation not in the Mike and Robin arsenal at the point of recording, notwithstanding Walter Gundy's harmonica. Perhaps he was just a friend who happened to be around at the recording, but Robin could play, and Mike more so, so let's assume that to be the reason.

The jug band feel of the song almost takes us back to Clive-era ISB: clattering washboard and Licky's solid guitar strum too. Certainly, you felt, this sounds like a band.

'Big Ted' left the sty a few months before the album, Elektra issuing it as a single, in the way of the time, not so much with a view to being a major seller, but as a taster for the album. This is the only song to be recorded in New York (the rest at Sound Techniques in London), which may be another reason for Gundy's presence. The B-side was 'All Writ Down': a song recorded at the same sessions, but not to see release for some time, and then on a different label to boot.

'White Bird' (Heron)

The album has but six tracks, and this is one of the two reasons why. Both Mike and Robin contributed long pieces taking up more or less 30 minutes of playing time. The amount of music you could fit on vinyl was in inverse proportion to the sound quality; the longer, the less quality fidelity: hence 'All Writ Down' being sidelined.

'White Bird' is Mike's long piece, concerning a journey through mystical lands to find… something. (Maybe what was being sought in Scientology?) It's actually a very beautiful piece, with some of Mike's finest guitar work holding it together, driven, where required, by Rose, and given substance by Licky on the organ, leaving Robin to flit between instruments to colour the sections and different melodies and tempos. I would venture that of the two long pieces; this is the most successful. Mike's voice is in superb form. The short instrumental interlude – where Mike's guitar duets with Robin's Chinese banjo (I suspect not it's true name – there are a number of instruments in China that use a stretched skin) – is perfection, as is the use of sarangi, with its sound richer than the gimbri, though it plays much the same lines. And finally, Robin's flute adds just the right floating quality. The success of the song is illustrated by the fact that it doesn't seem to be so long and never outstays its welcome.

The sleeve – on the back and inside of the gatefold – features paintings by Mike and Robin, illustrating their respective long pieces and incorporating some of the lyrics. Mike's features only a few lyric snippets.

That 'White Bird' never achieved the prominence of 'A Very Cellular Song', is a great shame. It deserved better. Long songs are difficult for up-and-coming bands. If you are playing a one hour set, then inserting two fifteen-minute pieces is a huge chunk out of the time. As the band grew in popularity and sets could be longer, that freedom may have opened them up to writing longer pieces.

'Dust Be Diamonds' (Heron/Williamson)

No, it's not a misprint; here is a joint composition. Plus, Mike makes his only appearance on a vibraphone! Why this was the only joint composition is unknown – Mike and Robin always maintained their own creative paths throughout. Was this song something one or the other couldn't finish, so the other came in and tied things up? We had certainly reached a point where they were both influenced by the other in terms of performance and style.

'Big Ted' is almost a Heron song, 'White Bird' almost a Williamson song. Well, debatable, but you get the drift. 'Dust Be Diamonds'... is a strange song and certainly moved into areas that were new. The verses have an almost lounge jazz feel, enhanced by the vibraphone, as Robin sings in a smooth, steady voice lacking the swooping histrionics he was capable of (I mean, cop his falsetto at the end of 'Big Ted'!). But then on the chorus, the tempo changes and it all goes strange, as the voice is followed note-for-note by Robin's electric guitar, going through effects pedals too, no less. There is also more excellent bass from Rose.

It would be fascinating to find out who wrote what here. For myself, I would have put this song after 'Big Ted', leaving the original vinyl to end side one with 'White Bird'. Still, in Joe Boyd we trust, and I assume he felt the released sequence worked best. See the final summing up for more on this.

'Sleepers, Awake!' (Heron)

The four-piece was the gift that kept on giving. As well as having a fuller sound – well, live at any rate – Mike was able to present this charming slice of a cappella with all four voices. It resonates with gospel tinges before falling into a path between children's song and doo-wop – which is all to the good. Younger readers may not realise how diverse music was post-1967. *Changing Horses* was in the album charts (reaching 30) with *Led Zeppelin II*, Tom Jones, Engelbert Humperdinck, Johnny Cash, *The Sound of Music*, and Cream. The album age was upon us, creating a different market to the increasingly teeny-angled singles. If reaching the 30s seems a weak showing for the ISB, it's because there was such high-selling competition. Anyway, the point is that things were not so compartmentalized, and plonking an a cappella in the middle of an album was fine. Live, ISB performed the traditional song, 'Bright Morning Stars', as an a cappella number, and that too sounded fine. It was credited to Mike, but in truth was trad. arr. Heron. Mike was obviously listening to Shaker hymns and southern gospel around this period.

'Mr. and Mrs.' (Williamson)

With most artists, you can take a track off an album and add it to the one before or the one after, and you'd not really see the join. The thing about 'Mr. and Mrs.' is that there's not a chance in a million that you could do that. No way would this gently mysterious near-pop song squeeze into *Wee Tam*, with the song's rippling electric guitar lines from Mike, Rose's bass underpinning, and both Robin and Licky tying things together with their organs (Yes, grow up). Robin also plays acoustic, and he and Mike bang and shake percussion, most notably on the jug-band-flavoured chorus. I'm told that there is some Scientology in the lyrics, what us mere mortals don't get, but to be fair, you don't have to 'get' that. It's a strange song. I like it for sure, but it would be a long way down the list of ISB songs I'd choose for a desert island.

'Creation' (Williamson)

So, Robin. Pick a simple subject for a long song. Creation? A bit complicated, *nes pas*? Well, I think I'll go for it anyway. Yes, it's Robin's long song for the album – another fifteen minutes. It's episodic, tied together with a kind of 'Volga Boatman' vocal chorus flowing through much of things. Ivan Pawle of Dr. Strangely Strange plays piano and organ (that band is sometimes referred to as The Emerald String Band, being Irish and treading similar paths to the ISB. Their three-and-a-bit albums are well worth seeking out. As an aside, in recent years, I knew I'd seen them play somewhere but couldn't remember anything about it. Until one Andy Roberts produced a picture of me jamming with the band informally in Leeds. Put it down to old age!).

For the first time on the album, Robin picks up the USP ISB (!) instruments of his: guitar, gimbri and violin. Likewise, Mike picks up the sitar, plays percussion, and makes a rare appearance on the mandolin. Rose and Licky add percussion, as well as bass (Rose) and kazoo (Licky). Looking at the lyrics in front of me now, I'm lost in lisping eyebrows and proof that oysters cry. I'm of the firm belief that you don't have to understand song lyrics, but you can just enjoy the flow and the sound. Well, verily, verily. Eventually, we reach the actual creation, as the seven days are narrated with the day's work. As usual, the mythologies seem to be drawn from no particular source but a grab-bag of wonder. Verily, verily.

So, we reach Russia as we cossack our way into a new part of the song where Loki – god of mischief – pops his head up to be naughty. And then we hit the drawled jazz-like 'amethyst galleon' section, which is the song's downfall. Where 'A Very Cellular Song' went out on a positive high, this finale just drags along far too long. At one point, it seems to stop but then reappears. Maybe by this time, the hippie listener had used the sleeve to prepare herbal niceties and had 'crashed out' before this bit. It's a shame: 'Creation' is a hell of a song – it just needed some editing. Still, with that, the horses had been changed, and it was time to gallop off to the next pasture.

Conclusion

Overall, this could have been a stronger album than was released. We know of other songs which were around at the time that could maybe have slotted in, with 'Mr. and Mrs.' and 'Dust Be Diamonds' sidelined. The aforementioned 'All Writ Down', 'Fine Fingered Hands' and 'See All The People' all would have made a more cohesive work which followed on more naturally from *Wee Tam and the Big Huge*. My thanks to Raymond Greenoaken for his fantasy tracklist for the album, which he put up on the excellent Facebook page Incredible String Band Discography, which is well worth your time, containing as it does, Rose Simpson, Stan Schnier, Graham Forbes and Annabelle Le Maistre (Malcolm's wife). These names will mean more as the book progresses.

I Looked Up (1970)

Personnel:
Robin Williamson: vocals, guitar, flute, gimbri, violin, percussion
Mike Heron: vocals, guitar (acoustic and electric), harpsichord, organ, piano
Licorice McKecknie: vocals, percussion, drums, hammer dulcimer, bass guitar
Rose Simpson: vocals, bass guitar, violin, percussion
With
Dave Mattacks: drums
Joe Boyd: producer
Record label: Elektra
Release date: April 1970
Chart position: UK: 30, US: 196
Running time: 41:22

And here we hit the point that showed the differing approaches of Mike and Robin. Here Mike contributes quite straightforward songs, catchy and poppy, at least two of which could have been pop material in the right hands. Of the six items here, Robin presents but two, both long, both difficult. Mini-skirted teens would not have bopped on *Top of the Pops* to Robin's contributions. Note also the relatively limited palette of instrumental textures: well, by ISB standards, perhaps. Some of the material here had been played at Woodstock – in retrospect, not the best choices for the occasion – but here is probably the most ignored album of the ISB's Elektra years. But look at the speed of output compared to modern musicians. We are mere months since *Changing Horses*, so it's a wonder that so much of this album is actually pretty damn good. But that was the way things were back then. I once chatted to Maddy Prior, and she admitted that Steeleye Span's original break-up was down to the endless treadmill of album, tour, album, tour. Mike told me during ISB's 21st-century revival that it was good to do some of these songs because in the past they hardly got to play them before it was time to promote the next album. Probably true, though some songs did endure – such as 'Everything Is Fine Right Now' – right to the end. This line-up even performed 'Empty Pocket Blues', for heaven's sake.

The sleeve is a colourful painting of dancing fairy folk, as more in the sky dangle a banner with the band's name on it. It was by American Janet Shankman, who would in due course become Mrs. Williamson, and is said to depict the perfect people from Scientology teachings. On the back are just the titles of the six songs contained within. Somehow, I had the American pressing. That sleeve featured a blurred picture of the band, Robin leaning behind on a door frame, knowing all. Mike smiles broadly: well, obviously. Rose wears a big red cowboy-type hat and a slightly native-American dress which could be made of chamois leather. Licky looks positively demure, her hair in corkscrew curls covered by a trilby with the brim turned down and a tweedy jacket. On the back were paintings of Robin and Mike with groovy stuff happening in the background and Rose and Licky in their own little circular bubbles. Check the photos to compare the two sleeves, and let the debate rage on!

The album charted, once again peaking at 30 in the UK, but no higher than 196 in the US. We can but wonder what that number would have been if Woodstock had been handled differently. The ISB set never featured on the Woodstock album, or the second Woodstock album, or in the film, or anywhere really. Steadily, the bits of film emerged, and at long last, in the 21st century, the music appeared on the eye-wateringly expensive anniversary multi-disc box set. I once again refer you to Rose for the full saga of Woodstock.

'Black Jack Davy' (Heron)

Young Davy makes his first appearance – he would return later. Although it's Mike's song, he takes mighty chunks from the traditional song known by many different titles – 'Seven Yellow Gypsies', 'Black Jack David', 'The Gypsy O' – but all follow the same storyline as here: Rich man's daughter or wife falls for a rough and free young man. She forsakes the wealth and finery – and a possibly much older husband from an arranged marriage – to live in the woods with him, and after a mostly fruitless search by husband or father, they live happily ever after. In some versions, Davy is killed for his cheek, while the wife or daughter ends it all rather than face life without him. So that's the lyrical content.

Mike pops the song into a major key (most traditional versions are in a minor) and gives it a jolly good sing-along feel. Here, Licky plays bass for the first time, while Rose plays fiddle alongside Robin. A simple, very folky line-up. The song would remain a stage favourite for many years.

'The Letter' (Heron)

Enter pop-rock Heron! In a sudden return to earlier album dynamics, only two of the band appear on this track: Mike on guitars, harpsichord and, of course, vocals; Rose on bass; the third player being the wonderful Dave Mattacks of Fairport Convention, on drums. Rose was in heaven, for the first time playing with a superb drummer like Dave. Mattacks had come up playing in strict-tempo dance bands before taking over the Fairport Convention drum stool from the sadly lost Martin Lamble. Mattacks stayed with them, off and on, for over 20 years or so. The session work he did – often with Dave Pegg on bass – was breathtaking, taking in Cilla Black, Nick Drake and anyone you could think of really.

'The Letter' is a terrific catchy little song, though not easily-coverable by others with its references to 'Mr. Heron' and letters from Rose's mother, but it rocks along in a way we hadn't heard the ISB do before. I mean, all rock references were essentially 1950s pastiches. This is just straight-ahead poppy, notwithstanding the slight change of melody for what we will call the middle eight (though it isn't in the middle and isn't eight bars long). So, was it that Robin and Licky were not going to contribute to such commercial stuff? Or was it simply they could see nothing to add? Who knows? I mean, both could have added something good to it, but would just have been tokenism, to say they were there? Either way, I can confirm that Rose's mother did write very reg-u-lar-lee, so that's alright then.

'Pictures In A Mirror' (Williamson)

If Mike's four songs on the album were lovely accessible melodic pieces, the two longer pieces by Robin were difficult – what was described as 'challenging' when a pupil of extreme behaviour was pointed out to me when I was supply teaching. In fact, ask any committed ISB fan to give the best example of a song which would not be a good introduction to the band, and they will wail 'Deeeeeeeep in the...': the opening line of the song. If last time out Robin had explored creation, here he was exploring reincarnation. Lord Randall is a name taken from a folk song of the same name, where Randall appears as a ghost, relating how his lady poisoned him. With eels, as you ask. Here though, Randall is incarcerated before being put to death, and soon after being reborn and in his mother's arms, while rapidly losing the memories of who he once was – rather like my ability to hold onto my dreams. It does all end on a slightly happier melodic note.

Musically, it's all rather deep and complex. Licky playing a descending shower of notes on the hammer dulcimer, opens proceedings. Rose rumbles beneath on bass, while Mike adds rather effective piano and organ. For the most part, Robin plays the violin: a neat little riff popping up all the time, counter-balanced by his guitar. In places, the fiddle hints slightly at the Eastern European vibe of 'Maybe Someday'. It all ends on strumming and percussion, which lets us all know that even if you're burned to death, you'll still come back as a bouncing breastfed baby in your mother's arms. Well, huzzah to that.

Recently, somebody brought up the subject of Robin's use of sexual allusions. Nipples like a berry appear here. My assumption is that Robin had soaked in the rural openness of British traditional songs (some traditional singers would not perform certain songs for collector, Maud Karples, as they 'weren't proper for a lady'). Add to that the country blues with its jelly rolls and diddy-wha-diddys, and the music hall with its 'Oh! What a beauty!', and you can understand the influences.

'This Moment' (Heron)

Another of the songs that the 21st-century ISB revived, which says a lot for its timeless quality. In a way, it's a more succinct form of 'Pictures In A Mirror', in that it says 'no matter how things are now, the next second will be different'. It's a simple instrumental line-up: Mike on guitar, Robin on lead acoustic guitar, Rose on bass and Licky on vocal. Oh, yes, Licky on vocal. As the song progresses, it makes your smile widen. Mike extemporizes on the 'Oh no' theme, including 'Gosh and golly no': a phrase popularised by British comedy actor Derek Nimmo, in the popular sitcom of the period, *All Gas and Gaitors*, where he played a young vicar. But back to Licky and her vocal, there's a point – a precious, joyous point – where she laughs while singing. Some bands may have done a retake, so thank you to (presumably) Joe Boyd for leaving it in to melt my heart every time I hear it. In many ways, this is another track that makes you feel that the ISB really was a four-piece at this time: everybody's part matters.

Incidentally, trivia fans, a line from the song that didn't make the recording is 'The grass beneath your feet is different'. For a while, a tape circulated called *Saturday Sun*, which was Witchseason trying to get other artists to cover the songs of their stable. Nick Drake's songs were there, and so was 'This Moment'. The performers were Elton John and Linda Thompson. I'm surprised it's never seen a commercial release. Also worth a mention is the folk trio, Saraband, whose only album, *Close To It All*, featured a rather lovely version of this song, as well as a version of 'Black Jack Davy', though they chose to credit it as traditional, interestingly, as it was certainly the Mike Heron take on the song. Mind, I do remember Roy Harper willfully singing Bob Dylan's 'North Country Girl' and announcing it as a traditional song: Dylan stole it.

'When You Find Out Who You Are' (Williamson)

Another of the songs performed at Woodstock, and definitely not exactly a repertoire shoe-in for such an event. Robin's second long, long song (of which life is, Tull fans), again, I'm told, taking Scientology theory by the horns. I don't know; to me, Robin was too deeply into things on this album, and the results mean he rambles where once he was concise. With Robin's guitar, Licky on drums, Rose on bass and Mike on piano, there isn't even a great deal of aural colour to see you through. It's not a bad song by any means; it just needed shaking up and to be made more three-dimensional. Again, that tightening may have made it shorter. What more can I say?

Well, I can say that Robin was again getting sexy. 'Remember, young man, when your love stick first rose between your legs?'. It doesn't even merit the phrase double entendre – it's single entendre. Mary Whitehouse may have needed smelling salts. Must we fling this filth at our psych-folk kids?

'Fair As You' (Heron)

What I can say is that this very, very lovely little song lifts the album at the end. It's unusual in that Rose and Licky sing the lead vocals as a duet (with occasional sections by Mike). It's gorgeous. Two female voices, which are not trained and mannered but just natural, are a treat. It's a trick that The Human League cottoned on to some years later. I wonder if those two also took inspiration from our heroines? And here, at least, the band uses its instrumental abilities to full effect. Robins nimble flute complements Mike's acoustic guitar, while Robin's gimbri is used to perfect effect. 'Fair As You' is so simple, yet so effective. It's an overlooked gem. And to some extent, so is the whole album.

Conclusion

So, it has to be said that if Robin had chosen just one of the long pieces and then written something a little more accessible, this may have been a better album for it. As it is, they overwhelm the charm of much of the album and make the whole lesser.

U (1970)

Personnel:
Mike Heron: vocals, sitar, piano, guitar, mandolin, organ, bass guitar
Robin Williamson: vocals, gimbri, flute, clay drums, guitar, bass guitar, mandolin,
12 string guitar, fiddle, jaws harp, washboard, shanai, soondri, electric guitar, voice
sitar, piano, drums
Rose Simpson: vocals, tabla, guitar, bass guitar
Licky McKechnie: vocals, spoons, drums, guitar
With
Janet Shankman: vocals, harpsichord
Peter Grant: banjo
Mal and Malcolm Le Maistre: vocals
Joe Boyd: producer
Record label: Elektra
Release date: October 1970
Chart position: UK: 34, US: 183
Running time: 1:47:07

U was basically Robin's idea to put together a multimedia piece, incorporating song, dance and a strong visual element. Mike went along with it, but played little part in its conception, it would appear. The dance element came from a new ensemble called Stone Monkey, put together by two gentlemen by the name of Rakis and Malcolm Le Maistre. We shall hear more of Malcolm later, as he became a member of the ISB, but here we get a taster, as he sings a section of Mike's 'Rainbow'.

The band met the two when they had encountered The Exploding Galaxy – another such outfit – while at the Chelsea Hotel in 1969, but subsequently, Rakis and Malcolm had left them to form Stone Monkey. To sort out details of how the piece would work, Stone Monkey moved into the row of cottages that the ISB now lived in, in Scotland: Glen Row by name. As a sideline here: I was with Mike in Leeds while a TV crew filmed him looking at a display of ISB photographs to comment on. He came to a picture of Glen Row, talked for a few moments on the cottages, then stopped and said, 'Oh wait, I still live there'. Glen Row consists of a row of joined cottages, and each band member had one, thus being together in the commune style but also having a level of privacy. The cottages were in a lovely rural setting, and there are a number of photographs of the band sledging, doing archery, smiling in the sunshine and so forth. After their previous communal living in Wales – which is seen in the *Be Glad For The Song Has No Ending* film – Glen Row must have seemed like a rather pleasant idyll.

If you want a one-sentence summary of what the piece was about, the album tells you: 'A surreal parable in dance and song'. Robin elaborated further: '...the vague notion was that a soul incarnates out of nowhere, lives, then vanishes again at the other end', which is where the title comes from: the clue is in the shape of the letter U. And, I suspect, clues are possibly all that people got from the piece in terms of 'plot'.

The show opened for a ten-day stint at London's Roundhouse on 8 April 1970, with the band and around a dozen dancers being the cast. The second run would be in the States, with six days at the Fillmore West: a notable hippie venue. The band funded this themselves, perhaps not the wisest financial move, as losses were so great that the final shows of the run had to dispense with Stone Monkey altogether. A rather poor quality film exists of the show: it had one recent cinematic showing with no further permission being granted by the various participants. Watching it, I got the impression that the music was rather wonderful, but the show itself seemed to amble, albeit in a rather charming way. It was rather like being a proud parent at the Christmas Nativity play: it was ramshackle but had your full support.

Thus the album: a way to try to get some of the money back. The show had run to some three hours on stage, and the double album would run to two. Joe Boyd booked them into a studio in San Francisco, and the band simply worked nonstop to record the album in just 48 hours. Hey, move over Pink Floyd; these boys and girls were sprinting. Reports say Mike or Robin would record their song, and the other would come in and overdub while the other slept. The thing is, you'd never know. My personal opinion is, it's one of a handful of double albums that justifies its length. Ask me to whittle it down to a single album, and I couldn't. Apart from a couple of theatrical pieces, every song makes sense in its own right, probably more sense than if you tried to fit it into a storyline. None of the playing sounds rushed or 'the first take will have to do'. It's a tribute to all four as musicians that they could achieve all this in 48 hours and on minimal sleep.

The album peaked at 34 in the UK album charts, though buying a double album was a mighty financial prospect back then and no doubt lowered sales. The gatefold cover was another of Shankman's paintings, not dissimilar to the one for *I Looked Up*, with characters forming the U shape. It was in keeping. On the back and inside were pictures of the ensemble on stage, giving Malcolm his first ISB sleeve appearance. The album's length meant it was some time before it appeared on CD, having to be a double CD. Readers may like to know that if you put it on in the car in Bradford, West Yorkshire, it'll allow you entertainment for the whole of your drive on A and B roads to the coast at Filey. I hope this information is useful.

'El Wool Suite' (Heron)

And we are off and seemingly back into familiar ISB territory, with Mike playing a quite stunning sitar solo. It's an instrumental, and a few moments in, Robin steps up the pace on clay drums with Rose on tabla. It's quite a lovely percussion arrangement as it goes. Mike speeds up the sitar, managing to make it rhythmic and melodic at the same time. Section three has an uncredited Indian harmonium drone, as Robin plays the bird with a flitting flute. Then it's a return to bouncy section two, with Rose somewhere in the mix on guitar.

El Wool is the planet on which *U* action takes place, as you ask. Assuming the sequence to be the same as the stage show, this must have been a mesmerizing opener, and you can almost see Stone Monkey dancing around the stage.

'The Juggler's Song' (Williamson)

Licky sings second vocal on this, and if your heart doesn't melt hearing her voice, you really need to see a doctor. 'Oooh, it's pretty!' Sigh. The backing is simple, with Robin on guitar, bass and mandolin. It's such a sweet little song and – like much of *U* – is entirely performable outside of the stage production. The various balls the juggler juggles, represent various elements and aspects of the universe. Even Robin almost slips into a Goon voice at one point, which adds to the joy of the piece.

And it ends with, essentially, a segue, with a mammoth dose of reverb, into the next piece, which is...

'Time' (Williamson)

A solo piece by Robin, with the man himself making a rare solo appearance on twelve-string guitar, coloured with mandolin. But the highlight of the song is his vocal, which swoops and soars and is as good as anything that graced the earlier albums. Though the concept of time no doubt fit the narrative, it in no way overpowers the song. Checking the sleeve, you might see somebody dressed as a clock. Well, once again, eat your heart out, Floyd and your clock-based musical shenanigans!

'Bad Sadie Lee' (Shankman)

Well, I said there might be a few pieces you could edit out, and most people – even the most devoted ISB fan – would probably pounce on this piece of nonsense. It's a parody/pastiche of every Hollywood cowboy song. You could probably add it to *Annie Get Your Gun* and nobody would notice. Mike gives it some barroom piano, no doubt with three fingers of whisky standing atop until some gunslinger shoots it off. Robin literally scrapes the fiddle, adding jews harp and washboard, while Licky and Rose add backing vocals, and Peter Grant adds suitable banjo. And above all this, Janet Shankman sings: the first time anybody outside the band took a lead vocal. It's either fun or annoying, depending on your point of view. Written by Janet Shankmen? Well that's exactly what the sleeve credit tells you, thus making it the first entire ISB song to be written by somebody outside of the band. In more recent years, Robin has hinted that he pretty much wrote it but was slightly embarrassed by it. I suspect the truth may very well lie between the two, and perhaps the credit should read Shankman/Williamson?

'Queen Of Love' (Williamson)

This has been long-regarded as one of Robin's finest pieces and was certainly a slightly different direction for the band. In parts, it's a very beautiful love song, very traditional in its structure. Robin plays guitar and bass while Janet plays harpsichord. Outside of that, Tom Constanton arranged an ensemble of players, which gives an almost classical feel to the piece, with flute, oboe, bassoon and other orchestral instruments. They flow in and out, helping the song along rather than taking it over. Of course, it is Robin, so there are changes of tempo and melody here and there, and again, sexual innuendo, as he plays 'three-legged man' (unless I misunderstand and it was a reference to the Isle of Man!) and 'seed thrower'.

I really can't hear Ms. Shankman's harpsichord, though I suspect it's in there somewhere.

The funny thing is, this is regarded as the high point of the album, but it wasn't actually in the show. Was that the original intention, that it should be on stage, but it was removed for timing and pace? Or maybe the album, sans dancers, needed another 10 minutes? I don't know. But I do know that if you want to introduce a non-believer into the church of Stringdom, this could be the lychgate through which to lead them. For me, it's strange that there weren't cover versions. I mean, it's as commercial as the likes of 'Windmills Of Your Mind' or 'MacArthur Park'. Maybe the three-legged man was too much for the non-underground listeners of the time.

'Partial Belated Overture' (Heron)

Mike is back in instrumental mode with another piece, I expect, for the dancers to work out to. The main point here is the lead is on a strident, slightly distorted electric guitar, courtesy of the Heron fingers, which he layers over some repeated piano figures. Rose plays the bass, and I really have to say that throughout the album, her bass-playing is superb. She claims she hardly knew what she was doing and just played what she was shown, but you don't play with the feel that she does if that's all you're doing. Okay, on this track, there is a need to give a good show, to allow the instruments to bounce off each other, but she does it. Meanwhile, Robin plays the fiddle and the shanai – an Indian double-reed instrument, an ethnic oboe if you will – with a powerful sound not far from Mike's electric guitar sound, and probably with not much less volume either. In fact, there are points where the two instruments are so similar in sound that it's hard to differentiate between the two.

And in those vinyl days, that was the end of side one.

'Light In Time Of Darkness'/'Glad To See You' (Heron/Heron)

Side two opened with Mike at the piano and Rose on the bass (see above), and as good an example as any of how Mike and Robin influenced each other. There's a Robin-esque feel to 'Light...' in Mike's vocal stylings. It certainly showcases his piano-playing talents, with little diverting instrumental fills popping up here and there. Mike's voice soars and uses dissonant techniques in places: a dangerous trick, as it can just sound out of tune, but here doesn't. In contrast, the simplicity of 'Glad To See You' is the lift at the end. It's here that

Rose's walking bass line enters and adds a whole new dimension to the lengthy solo piano and voice preceding. If there weren't hippie dancers greeting each other during 'Glad To See You', there damn well should have been.

'Walking Along With You' (Heron)

Rose has such an attractive naive voice that you wonder why there was not more use made of it. Here she takes the lead vocal in a charming style that feels like anyone might sound while singing as they walk along (with you). Mike's trademark guitar chording drives things along nicely. I assume the uncredited piano is by Mike, but it could just as easily be Robin, who is credited with bass. Again, some lovely chord progressions, going where they are not really supposed to, climbing and climbing in a direct semi-tonal cascade. I adore this track. And obviously, so does Rose, as it was one of the tracks she asked me to play when I last interviewed her for one of my radio programmes. 'There are many things will give you a good time/I have known a few', she sings. But the best is the simple pleasure of walking along with you. Amen.

'HiremPawnitof' (Heron)/'Fairies' Hornpipe' (Trad. Arr. ISB)

Well, here's the next silly song, which was no doubt a hoot live. In fact, it does work on record, though there are obvious points where there is a visual element missing. But it tells a tale, which no doubt either fit the narrative or made it even more baffling. Still, it's very jolly and very attractive, probably falling in the same camp as 'Log Cabin Home In The Sky' and 'Black Jack Davy', but suffering by comparison. It's a very folky lineup: Mike plays guitar and mandolin, Robin plays a folky fiddle, Licky rattles away on the spoons and Rose adds the bass. It all culminates in the traditional instrumental 'Fairies' Hornpipe' – the first recorded example since the first album, though in later days, the jigs and reels would become a major feature of the stage shows. In fact, I would say that this is the most obvious show tune number on the album. The lyrics follow the actions, men sing in shrill girls' voices, Robin proclaims in an actor type of way about enlightenment, and the whole song ends on the ludicrous line about 'happily growing cows'. Okay, yes, I like it. There. Said it.

'Bridge Theme' (Heron)

More of the instrumental-rock-meets-the-world-music, with Mike rocking out on both lead and rhythm electric guitars, as Robin adds the ethnic touch of shanai and soondri, pretty much following the paths an electric guitar would tread. Licky takes the drum stool, playing along with Rose's bass. There's nothing to fault the short piece. It is what it is, a bridge that leads to...

'Bridge Song' (Heron)

Now it's time for Licky to take the lead vocal. Boy, can she sing high. It's tempting to say that only dogs would hear parts of this song. Yet, Lickydoesn't miss a note. Oh sure, you think she will, it seems certain, like watching a car slide on ice, but she holds it, and it is a thing of beauty. There's a bit near the end where she and Mike are singing 'See you', and Licky is really – I mean really – really high. And then she goes up higher.... Just wow!

'Astral Plane Theme' (Williamson)
Robin solo on acoustic guitar. This is an instrumental illustrating just how much of a guitarist he is. You can hear so much in there, not least the using of the guitar as you would an oud: the runs on the lower strings are a trademark Williamson thing, and we know of this already. But here he is, sparkling up the top as well. As a piece, it probably uses so many ideas that most guitarists would have gotten five instrumentals out of it.

'Invocation' (Williamson)
If side two of the vinyl was Mike's slice of the album, then side three was Robin's. And here he is alone, just his voice, but with the addition of 'Greg Heats voice sitar'. It is precisely what the title tells you it is: an invocation to invite spirits. Did I say it's just Robin's voice? Well, that's what the sleeve says, but there is for sure a violin and gimbri in there, possibly even a bit of piano. And the voice sitar, I hear you ask? Well, the effect is to add echo, drone and sympathetic humming to the voice. These days, five minutes in the digital suite would give much the same effect. But back then, it was a thing of wonder. Funnily enough, the piece didn't die with the ISB, and when Robin wrote the music for The Mabinogi theatrical piece in Wales, he dusted it off. The Mabinogi is one of the great Wales sagas. It was even shown on TV, and a friend who was visiting couldn't believe that I would rather stay in and watch it than come down the pub. 'Invocation' was also performed at Woodstock, so did it predate *U* or was *U* in the planning stages back then?

'Robot Blues' (Williamson)
Funny song three, I suppose. It's just Robin on piano, showing a real skill at playing blues piano: a previously unsuspected skill. In fact, Robin's keyboard work has never really been exploited. Perhaps, like me, he couldn't be fussed with carting round yet another huge lump of musical equipment. The song tells the tale of randy robots fighting for the attention of a lady robot. It's full of innuendo, as befits such blues songs: pistons fill with oil, and pump-action is offered. It's 'Rocky Raccoon' in electronics. Lovely stuff, if a little light.

'Puppet Song' (Williamson)
Robin swaps back to guitar for another solo piece of storytelling. A jolly little tune pushes along the story of a man, a little man, who wants to work out who is in charge. He works his way up through politicians and kings and is passed along to the next one on every occasion, ending up with god, up a rickety ladder. And there is the answer. Or not. Nobody is in charge; we create our own path. Or something.

'Cutting The Strings' (Williamson)

Nobody but Robin would open a song with a long melody line that takes in every musical note known to mankind. If we had heard a couple of years previously that, 'We are all still here, no one has gone away' ('Job's Tears'), here we find, 'There now, they've all gone', as an opening line.

So, it's a waltz of sorts and probably not the most successful track: it stops, starts again, and feels like a sort of stoned show tune, which it may very well have been. Robin takes the lions share of the work on guitar, mandolin, gimbri, fiddle and flute. Licky sings and Mike plays sitar. Somebody – we know not who – bangs some hand drums.

'I Know You' (McKechnie)

Blimey! Licky writes her own song and performs it solo on guitar. Her voice stays relatively low here and just sounds superb. Her guitar-playing is adequate and the song is good, on the level of a folk club floor spot by an English Lit undergraduate. And winged people are mentioned – winged people featured more and more in the ISB from here on in. It was actually rather wonderful to hear that Licky was writing, and this skill would develop further throughout the rest of her tenure with the band.

'Rainbow' (Heron)

The finale. Rainbows were big in those days; even the flipping Rolling Stones sang about them (at the moment of writing, used in a TV commercial!) and decided that 'sh'e was a rainbow. I simply adore the initial piano and organ-led early part of 'Rainbow', initially sung by Mal from the dancers, who then hands over to Malcolm Le Maistre: for it is he making his vocal debut with ISB. If you sit me at a piano, sooner or later, I'll play the opening sequence. Ere long, Malcolm would be in that seat till the bitter end, and beyond in fact.

Then it's into a linking instrumental section before the main melody reappears with a choir of all six voices. Mike also plays guitars and bass, while Robin plays drums, soondri, fiddle, flute and mandolin. But Rose also plays bass and Licky also plays drums, so, rhythm section overkill somewhere. Anyway, Licky takes lead vocals before the whole thing explodes into a gospel-style declamatory finale, which probably goes on too long – would I be right in thinking this was the equivalent of the pantomime finale? – then it stops. But then, it's back with Mike singing sweetly to his organ accompaniment, before he gives it some screaming emotion, and we are into the coda and a jolly singalong of 'I have seen you there' from the ladies of the ensemble. Again, it probably goes on too long given its simplistic structure, but it again allowed tout ensemble to dance around the stage. It's like the finale of the pantomime, where everybody comes down the stairs, all singing and dancing together.

Conclusion

So, can you enjoy the album without seeing the show? Yes. Can you see the show? Well, not really. A rather poor quality film exists, but it's never been given permission for release, nor has the will and the money been offered to clean it up digitally. Oh well, as Peter Green once said. And it is at this point that we say farewell to Elektra Records. Of Joe Boyd's Witchseason bands, the ISB had been the one not to be on Island Records: the label that Chris Blackwell had formed. Next time, new projects, new label, same ISB.

Be Glad For The Song Has No Ending (1971)

Personnel:
Robin Williamson: guitar, bass guitar, fiddle, hand percussion, gimbri, keyboards, mandolin, sarangi, vocals
Mike Heron: guitar, bass guitar, chimes, glockenspiel, harp, horn, keyboards, sitar, vocals
Licorice McKechnie: vocals, keyboards, fiddle
Rose Simpson: vocals, bass guitar, percussion
Joe Boyd: producer
Record label: Island
Release date: March 1971
Chart position: UK: -, US: -
Running time: 50:19

And so, the band bade farewell to Elektra Records and settled in at Island Records. The majority of Joe Boyd's Witchseason acts had been placed on Island: John Martyn, Nick Drake, Fairport Convention and so on. So it was the ISB joining the rest of the stable, though as this was the last time Joe Boyd would produce the band, it was perhaps a pyrrhic victory. And it really is hard to imagine what Island thought when they were presented with the band's first album offering. It was, as Joe Boyd said, a clearing out of the cupboards. Some tracks went back as far as *Wee Tam and the Big Huge*, some were live tracks, and Rose and Licky made sporadic appearances because of the dates spanned. The clearing out also accounts for the real mix of styles, going from the real hippie cascades of a few years before to the more rock approach, which would increasingly become the ISB style for the rest of their career. The whole of the second vinyl side was instrumental, from the film which shares the album's title and of which we shall speak ere long. All in all, there's much to love on the tracks here, but as an overall piece, it is very fractured. If you want a comparison, The Beatles' *Yellow Submarine* album – which consisted of old tracks, new tracks and film instrumentals – is a shoe-in.

And so, the film. It was, effectively, two films joined at the hip. The first part was essentially a documentary featuring the band in full hippie mode. Mike and Rose walk around at their cottage – at Roman Camps between Edinburgh and Glasgow – looking like Beatrix Potter characters, and Mike sits being interviewed, as dutiful Rose attends to her needlework and stays quiet in the background. I think Rose's book will tell you much more about that image. Certainly, it describes life at the small former miners' cottage, surrounded by the spoil heaps where the pits had spewed out their contents. Robin tips his hat and introduces himself as 'genius of this parish' – well, of course. Robin also wanders along with Licky and the dog, Leaf, visiting an instrument maker and playing an electric guitar with a spanner in a bottleneck style, though Elmore James certainly does have nothing on this baby!

There's a couple of live-in-the-studio performances from the four-piece ISB: 'All Writ Down' making a reappearance from it's single release (thus making it a song released in much the same form, if not exactly the same take, on both Elektra and Island). There's also live concert footage from The Royal Albert Hall in 1968. Sadly, this material only exists in short clips, so those who think there may be a whole 1968 concert out there are in for a sad time. What we get are bits of 'A Very Cellular Song' and 'Mercy I Cry City': the latter proving that Robin did indeed play whistle and harmonica at the same time. The film concludes with a dramatic mime and music piece with no dialogue, known by a few names, but usually as 'The Pirate and the Crystal Ball'. In a sense, it's perhaps a tighter version of *U*, as the Stone Monkey dancers – errr – dance, and the band and friends, act. Essentially, the pirate – played by Rakis – half inches the crystal ball from the Fates: portrayed by Licky, Rose and Melanie Schofield (she of the vocals on *U*'s 'Rainbow', and commemorated after her death in Robin's song, 'Fare Thee Well Sweet Mally'). Anyway, the Fates are put out by this and summon Herne the Hunter: a woodland god brought to public attention in the TV series *Robin of Sherwood* some years later. Herne is played here by Malcolm Le Maistre, who leaps lively through the fields, tripping over in the process, but it's left in the film because, well, why not, man? He captures the pirate and thrusts him in front of two gods: played by Mike and Robin in enough make-up to keep Max Factor in business for a year – or maybe two years in fact. Their abode appears to be a curtain warehouse which somebody has attacked with baking foil. It's schizophrenic nirvana. Actually, I may be being over-cynical here.

The film was made over one weekend, probably with virtually no budget, and in fact, is quite charming viewing – if you can put your head back to those years. Anyway, back at the plot: the gods sentence the pirate to an eternal cycle of reincarnation, as we see lots of images, supposedly of the pirate's life (including the Welsh farmer who owned Big Ted, I believe) and the whole thing ends on the sound of a baby crying.

Unlike *U*, you can see the results. The film was cleaned up and released on VHS a few years ago, and I believe it's available on DVD. And actually, it's worth the watch, the more so given how little of the ISB was captured on film. Oh, and there's a reading of the list of instruments the ISB are taking on stage, including the Paul McCartney bass – so 'that' was still there at that time. And Mike puts orange peel on to look like a duck, as Robin slips a mask on. And it's lovely. What happened to being childlike? Now so much is child-'ish'. Anyway, that's the film. Here's the record.

'Come With Me' (Williamson)
Despite being called a soundtrack album, things kick off with a song not in the film. It's a typical Robin song: mystical without being specific. As happened often, there are instruments not mentioned: here, recorders and flute appear to be present. I would say, Rose: recorder; Robin: flute. Just a guess.

The vocals are a duet, with Robin and Licky largely in the stratosphere. There's a choral a cappella section that stresses green credentials: valleys, seas and so on must be conserved. Considering it's Robin, the song is strongly structured and doesn't outstay its welcome. In a less fractured setting than the album, this would be an absolute gem; perhaps not up there with 'Maya', but very close.

'All Writ Down' (Heron)
So here is the song we heard before as a B-side and is featured in the film. Robin plays lead on what you would take to be an electric guitar unless you see the film. But it's an acoustic, played through the pick-up. It's a poppy little number which would seem to be the tale of a young lad introduced into the joys of the bedroom by a cougar. It's perhaps a little icky to modern ears, as the lad is described as a 'little school boy'. She then casts him aside, much to the lad's chagrin. In time he decides that this was actually the best way. Well, that's what it sounds like, but I have heard it said it's another reference to Scientology. 'Every cell of my body has it all writ down' is a direct reference to Scientology, but..., look, as a songwriter myself, it hardly matters – take it as you will. The main thing here is Mike's more rock approach against Robin's whimsy. Indeed Mike would be credited as just Heron before long. But that's for later.

'Veshengro' (Williamson)
Another excellent Robin song that appears to allude to reincarnation. It's also Robin solo, and again, it doesn't appear in the film. It's not a groundbreaker, but it's as good a song as you can wish for, lost in the grab-bag of this album. It has the trademarks, the changes of melodic structure, and some fine guitar work from Robin.

Like the opening track, this is overlooked because the album as a whole is overlooked. Neither Mike nor Robin appear to have revisited anything from this album post-ISB. A shame, in my view.

'See All The People' (Heron)
This dates back a few years and was recorded live (you can hear somebody knocking the microphone just before the vocals). Mike and Robin duet on guitars, Robin doing some pretty astonishing lead runs throughout. The words, however, are either charmingly hippie or toe-curlingly embarrassing. 'See all the people laugh, ha hahahaha' and 'cry, boo hoo, boo hoohoohoo'. I mean, I'm not going to prescribe which side you should fall on. I used to go out with a lady who would just start laughing on hearing this song: not in mockery; she simply found it funny. Fair enough. I would be overjoyed to write a song that made people spontaneously laugh. Some of Mike's funny songs missed the mark: cf. 'Frutch', later in the book, but earlier than here.

Above: Mike and Robin in the very early days looking like medieval troubadours on the way to hippy threads. It was during this period that Mimi and Mouse would dance with the band. (*Alamy*)

Left: The UK sleeve of the debut album showed the trio with a range of exotic instruments which never appeared on any album by the band. (*Elektra*)

Right: The US release of the debut album with Mike looking somewhat more hip than on the UK sleeve. Quite what Clive was wearing is hard to put into words. (*Elektra*)

Left: After *Sgt Pepper*, *5000 Spirits* has to be the most iconic album sleeve to emerge from the Summer of Love. It was designed by The Fool - artists and clothes designers in residence at Apple. (*Elektra*)

Right: The rear of *5000 Spirits* sees Mike and Robin looking very 'happy' as they hide in the undergrowth surrounded by more artwork from The Fool. (*Elektra*)

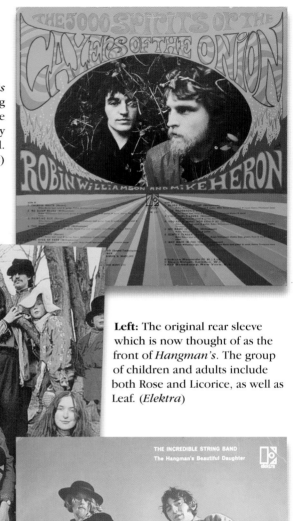

Left: The original rear sleeve which is now thought of as the front of *Hangman's*. The group of children and adults include both Rose and Licorice, as well as Leaf. (*Elektra*)

Right: The original front cover, which later became the rear of *Hangman's*, seemed to perfectly reflect the music within; blue skies and nature, but with a feeling of chill lurking somewhere. (*Elektra*)

Left: *Wee Tam and The Big Huge* was issued both as a double album and as two singles. The photos of the pair looking divine in Frank Zappa's garden formed the inner sleeve / rear sleeve with the lyrics on the front. The CD releases have usually seen this reversed. (*Elektra*)

Right: The back, later front, of *The Big Huge* with the boys in full hippy mode of floppy hats, ruffled shirts and beads. (*Elektra*)

Left: The use of the lyrics as the front cover of *Wee Tam* boldly stressed that the words were important, an emerging concept post-*Pepper*. (*Elektra*)

Right: The front, later back cover of *Big Huge*. (*Elektra*)

Left: The *Changing Horses* cover was the first to feature Rose and Licorice as part of the band, with the four festooning a tree in a park in America. (*Elektra*)

Above: In many respects, the band's appearance at Woodstock was a massive misfire when it could have been the lift into another level of stardom. That said, what film and audio that has been released are excellent from a performance point of view.

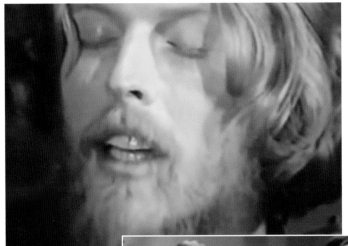

Left: Mike always seemed the most rooted of the two, with his sturdy good looks, while Robin gave out a sense of otherworldliness and an impression that he could see something that you couldn't.

Right: The ISB made a couple of appearance on the Julie Felix show on BBC2. Here they are in full hippy pomp, playing 'The Half Remarkable Question'.

Left: Here the boys join with Julie Felix herself for a spirited rendition of 'Painting Box'. While this appearance exists, the other one, featuring the much rarer 'Fine Fingered Hand', has not come to light.

Right: Mike performing 'All Writ Down' in the *Be Glad* film, which featured both live and studio performances by the band.

Left: Robin Williamson, 'Genius of this parish' in the *Be Glad* film, during one of the studio performances.

Right: Rose Simpson on the iconic Hofner violin bass. Purportedly the bass was borrowed from Dave Pegg and never returned. Rose believes it may now be owned by Stevie Winwood.

Left: Mike on the Gibson bass in the early seventies. On the performance of 'Everything Is Fine Right Now', Mike would play the solo on the bass, with Robin joining on mandolin.

Right: Robin's Leven guitar was sanded down at some point and he illustrated it with inks. No photos have been found giving a clear colour view of the illustrations on the guitar.

Left: Rose playing the mandolin. Although her role within the band was primarily as bass player, she was also featured at various points on fiddle, guitar, keyboards and tabla alongside other percussion and, of course, vocals.

Right: The ISB rarely made it onto television screens, but this photo captures a German TV appearance with Licky playing guitar. In this case, she playing Robin's illustrated Lowden.

Left: The four-piece version of the band performing 'Everything Is Fine Right Now', again from German TV, with Rose at the keyboard while Mike takes bass duties on the Gibson SG that had replaced the Hofner violin bass.

Right: Licky looking very demure with neat hair, dark clothing and an enigmatic smile. Her influence on the band was subtle but profound.

Left: Janet Shankman became the cover artist for *I Looked Up*. It may have invoked the bright colours of *5000 Spirits*, but it was less successful in its execution. (*Elektra*)

Right: The US release of *I Looked Up* dispensed with the Janet Shankman painting and replaced it with this photograph of the band in double exposure and with the ladies to the front. (*Elektra*)

Left: Ms Shankman was once more at the helm for the sleeve of *U*. Its greater simplicity provided a more satisfying image. (*Elektra*)

Right: The rather underwhelming cover of the band's first release for the Island label showed stills from the *Be Glad* film with some rather dated graphics which scream The Seventies. (*Island*)

Left: *Liquid Acrobat* is considered by many to be the last truly classic ISB album, and its title and understated sepia sleeve reflect that they were still the band that had been a mystical 60s entity. (*Island*)

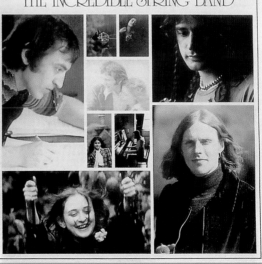

Right: The last of the hippy trimmings were cast aside for the sleeve of *Earthspan,* showing the band in 'smart casual' mode. (*Island*)

Left: For many, the sleeve of *No Ruinous Feud* was a betrayal of all that had gone before, with only Malcolm looking slightly like the hippy image they were leaving behind. (*Island*)

Right: *Hard Rope and Silken Twine*, the final album by the original band, attempted to regain a little whimsy in its sleeve art. (*Island*)

Left: Mike's first solo album went out of its way to make a bold statement. It screamed, 'This isn't the ISB, this is something new and brasher.' It's all silver foil and cartoon speech bubbles. And a pineapple. (*Island / Elektra*)

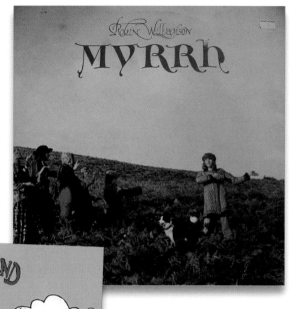

Right: In complete contrast to Mikes brash sleeve, Robins solo album *Myrrh* extended the rural theme of the ISB and retained a feeling of mysticism with its hand gestures. (*Edsel*)

Left: The revived band, without Robin, produced two albums which were essentially live re-recordings of past glories, surprisingly containing much the same songs on both. (*Quadrant*)

Right: Like its predecessor, the second of the 21st-century releases again featured a naive style of sleeve art. (*Secret Records*)

Left: Robin eventually returned to the UK after a period of living in the USA. Today his primary instrument has become the Celtic harp and he remains the most active of the former band members.

Right: Mike has changed little over the years. His dark hair may be thinner, but the perma-smile is still present.

Left: Musically, Rose Simpson moved off the radar after she left the ISB. She hit the news when she became Mayoress of Aberystwyth and it was discovered by the press that she played Woodstock. In 2020 she published her autobiography covering her time with the ISB to great approval.

Right: Mike has, over the years, become an icon to younger musicians. His tours with the likes of Trembling Bells and his autobiography have kept the flame alive.

Left: Undoubtedly much of the band's success and recorded perfection is down to Joe Boyd, producer extraordinaire. Boyd has worked with so many greats, including Nick Drake, Fairport Convention, Pink Floyd and John Martyn.

Right: Robin is still a creative force to be reckoned with producing songs, writings and artwork, as well as touring solo or with his wife Bina.

Live at the Fillmore
THE INCREDIBLE STRING BAND
1968

Left: Another surprise appearance from the archives was this album, recorded by a radio station for live broadcast of the band playing at the Fillmore in 1968. The sound quality is low fi, but it is still a fascinating snapshot of the band at the time. (*Hux Records*)

Right: This double CD was a package of two albums previously released separately. One is a live concert from Canada which features the short-lived lineup with Gerard Dott. The second CD, *The Chelsea Sessions*, consisted of demos and alternate takes from the sessions before the recording of *5000 Spirits*. (*Talking Elephant*)

robin williamson & mike heron

bloomsbury 1997

Left: The first inkling of the revival of the band came in the form of the 1997 concerts. Mike and Robin insisted that all publicity should use their names and not that of the ISB. The Bloomsbury concert was recorded and released. (*Pig's Whisker*)

'Waiting For You' (Williamson)
Robin in amusing pseudo-ragtime 1920s 'boopboopee doo' mode, and for me personally, the most entertaining song on the album. This is the song that Rose bows out with, after being introduced as Miss Finola Bum Garner in a silly introducing-the-band segment, which always makes me smile, and also brings to mind The Bonzo Dog Doo Dah Band's 'The Intro And The Outro'. In fact, Robin's spoken interjections throughout the song (incidentally the longest piece on the song part of the album) are always lovely and don't grow old with repeated listening. The band's eclectic nature – dipping into whatever music style they fancied – was becoming an increasing feature; indeed, in the latter stages, some would accuse them of doing something just because they can. But here, it's all very lovely. In many ways, I can think of no nicer way to hear Rose for the last time with the ISB: everyone happy, everyone smiling.

'The Song Has No Ending (Parts 1 to 9)' (Williamson/Heron)
There is no over-arching theme here, no single piece with branches looping off. Essentially, it's a number of tunes joined together, with no vocals, save chanting and 'la la' type stuff. The credits simply say that the whole band play the instruments for which they are known, which outside of sitar and fiddle, probably means little. It's mostly in a world music style, hinting at Russia in the opening part, an Indian raga here, West Indian music there. There's even 'Beyond The See' from *Wee Tam*, nestling in amongst the things. I often wondered how that worked. Were the songs and tunes the property of Warlock: Witchseason's music publishing arm? Very probably, but the performance was the property of Elektra, no? Maybe it's a new performance or a subtle remix that can be claimed to be so. Given that soundtrack music is often a bit of a drag without the film to go with it, it's quite a feat that this is a very listenable 20 minutes or so – to my mind, preferable to either side two of *Yellow Submarine* or (Gasp!) *Tubular Bells*. It's varied and inventive, and the performance and execution are as excellent as you would expect. When seen within the film, it works. But it also works independently too. Of course, if you've seen the film as many times as I have, you can't help but run it in your head as you listen: Rakis has just fallen over in that meadow; Mike is swirled in joss stick perfume; Rose and Licky look lovely with leaves for headdress, and so on.

This may not have been the album that Island had hoped for, but taken for its individual parts, it's a damn fine listen. I think – with a few tweaks and a much better cover – this could have been a truly classic album; well, at least on a par with *Changing Horses* and *I Looked Up*. Maybe someday I should do a mix tape of these three albums as I feel they should have been? Anyway, this is a hidden gem – find it. Don't dismiss it.

Liquid Acrobat As Regards The Air (1971)

Personnel:

Robin Williamson: oud, whistle, cymbals, acoustic and electric guitars, violin, cello, oboe, mandolin, kazoo, bass guitar, bass recorder, banjo, flute, vocals

Mike Heron: organ, sitar, electric and acoustic guitars, piano, harmonium, bass guitar, electric piano, flute, vocals

Lickie McKechnie: harmonium, drums, organ, bass guitar, kazoo, pipe organ, spoons, bodhran, autoharp, vocals

Malcolm Le Maistre: harpsichord, drums, bass guitar, kazoo, swanee whistle, percussion, mandolin, whistle, tenor recorder, bouzouki, glockenspiel, harmonica, clarinet, church organ, vocals

With

Stan Lee: pedal steel guitar, bass guitar

Gerry Conway: drums

Stanley Schnier: producer

Record label: Island

Release date: October 1971

Chart position: UK: 46, US: 189

Running time: 48:29

If the switch to Island Records was going to take place at any point, this should probably have been the point: and in some respects, perhaps it was. While *Be Glad...* had proven to be a pleasing-enough rag-bag of things from the dressing up box, here was a shiny new String Band: hair slicked down and tie neatly done up. Well, perhaps not. But this is certainly the album that lifted the ISB into a more rock-orientated approach while retaining the eclectic beauty of what had gone before, and indeed, the instrumentation, to a large extent. Rose had left the band, ostensibly to become a sound engineer, though other things got in the way, and again, I refer you to her book for full details.

In Rose's stead, Malcolm Le Maistre was drafted in. He had, of course, sung on *U* and appeared on the *Be Glad...* cover and in the film. So rather in the way of Rose and Licky, Malcolm's had been a steadily converging path. If he was brought in to take over Rose's bass duties, it's little in evidence here, with all four taking to the lower-register four-string instrument and even farming it out to Stan Lee: actually, Stan Schnier working under a pseudonym. As an American, technically, he may not have been allowed to work as such. Stan is another satellite person who would become a full-time String in the future. There was also Gerry Conway playing the drums on one track. Gerry would later take the stool behind Fairport Convention, but up at this point, he had worked through Eclection, Fotheringay and Cat Stevens and was – along with Dave Mattacks and Timi Donald – the go-to drummer for folk rock luminaries.

This was the album that saw a more rock approach. Was this lead by Mike, who on this album was credited as Heron while the rest were still on first-name terms? It's believed this was to give him a more rock image. Mike had a solo album, which featured John Cale of The Velvet Underground, and all of The Who: well, Townsend and Moon with Ronnie Lane of the Faces on bass at any rate, and we will have a look at that in due course. On the single was Jimmy Page. More of this, too, in a later chapter, but suffice to say, Mike/Heron was up for rocking out. Of course, this may have been to do with Scientology, whose philosophy was to present yourself in a better, more successful and open way. So a move toward a more accessible style of music would have fit in with that.

As a side note, this was the first version of ISB I saw perform live. I was mesmerized by Licky's voice, and the whole package stirred an excitement in my soul that never left me. Which is why I am writing this book, but you probably guessed that. I'll tell you more about the live experience in the concluding chapter.

Most would consider this the best of the ISB Island albums. For a start, Mike and Robin are both happy inhabiting a middle ground. As time passed, this would be a widening area, but here it's a happy blend.

Malcolm's role in the band came as seamless, though his vocals are less in evidence than would be imagined. As he tells it, he was a dancer with a little musical ability, but the band thrust instruments into his hands and he diligently learned his part. On stage, he would increasingly be an amusing front man as Mike and Robin swapped instruments and tuned up. Equally, Licky was now taking a larger part in the band, both instrumentally, in the writing, and as a vocalist. Her soaring voice is more restrained, and the better for it.

Overall, this is one hell of an album, which doesn't grow old or tired. Indeed, it repays every listening.

'Talking Of The End' (Williamson)
Opening with oud, whistle, and sitar from Mike coming in, there was still much of the distinctive ISB sound we knew and loved. Robin's vocals were more precise now, holding sweet melody, rather than rushing up and down simply because he could, again, perhaps the 'being more accessible' philosophy. But there was still the changing of pace and melody lines, including a truly beautiful sitar and guitar duet. And then, a pedal steel guitar! I remember thinking at the time; this was some form of blasphemy. I mean, yes, I was a little more closed-minded about music back then, so to me, pedal steel equalled country-and-western equalled rhinestones and stetsons, and I hated all that with the vigour that only the young crusader can summon. I mean, it rivalled my dislike of my dad's Frank Sinatra albums.

But back to the ISB. Listening now, it works. It's a gentle and lilting respite from the mystic to the love. It's haunting and just right. And introducing new instruments and using them in different ways was the heart of the ISB, right?

'Dear Old Battlefield' (Williamson)
Robin was certainly embracing a far more 'commercial' strand of music: more mainstream, less magical, but hey, we all change. I first heard this song on

John Peel's radio programme. I was at my grandma's house, and she did the
usual tutting and 'they can't write proper tunes anymore' thing that grandmas
born in 1904 were wont to do. (Mind you, her major venom was reserved for
Supertramp and 'Bloody Well Right', which was profanity beyond the pale!)

Anyway, this, I would say, is the ISB's first full-on electric track, though
you might say 'The Letter' (though that was watered down by harpsichord
flourishes). At any rate, it's certainly the first Robin full-on electric. I mean, it's
hardly Sabbath, but Robin and Mike both play electric guitars – Mike on lead
– and there's bass and drums and keyboards, so yeah: the standard rock line-
up. Lyrically, it may not be 100% straightforward, but it appears to be anti-war
(In rock songs, name a pro-war song?!?! I mean, even Sabbath with War Pigs!),
and musically, it stays on one tune and tempo from start to finish. Scientology
is in there for sure: 'If not for the plan of the magic man who finally leads us
out of the woods' – L. Ron Hubbard himself, I believe – and 'death is unreal'
are both very direct. When I listened on the radio, with granny clucking in the
background, I was won over. And I remain so to this day.

'Cosmic Boy' (McKechnie / Heron)
Okay, so it's hippie girl lyrics. Okay, so it's slightly twee. But do I look bothered?
No. This piece is performed as a duo, Mike playing some truly lovely rolling
piano. The tune hints at ragtime and Edwardian parlour tunes, and slows to
hit the lyrics. And Licky sings it perfectly. She has a voice inflexion and accent,
which is unique. Writing this, it occurs to me that I don't recall ever hearing her
speak. So, I asked Rose, who told me that of the four members when she was
there, Licky had by far the strongest Scottish accent. So now you know.

But nobody did, or does, sing like her, and when she uses her voice on a
song like this – not requiring her to hit wine-glass-shattering levels – it really is
lovely. No hippie boy could help wishing that he was that cosmic boy. Lovely.
Oh, and a joy to test your piano chops with. I used it as a rehearsal piece on
many occasions. I never tried to sing it, mind.

'Worlds They Rise and Fall' (Heron)
Mike in love song mode is a thing to behold, and this medium-paced gem
fulfils all you need in that department. Over an acoustic guitar rhythm base,
with effective chordal piano stabs punctuating things, it's bright and heartfelt.
It's made more effective by slower sections over the organ, with Licky's voice
used to great effect. At a little over three minutes in length, it says what it needs
to, and then leaves. It certainly, to me, reiterates the Scientology cause, striving
for a more open and commercial feel – for better or worse, depending on your
view.

'Evolution Rag' (Williamson)
Mandolins and calliope-sounding organ drive along this jolly bit of ragtime,
with lyrics about, well, evolution. But you probably guessed that. Slight it may

be, but it always raises a smile. I mean, 'air croquettes'? Wonderful. There was also mucho kazoo shenanigans going on. Actually, listening now over the ISB's body of work, the kazoo features little throughout (this is its last appearance on an ISB record), while the more casual listener, I believe, thinks it was a constant. It's 'play it again Sam' all over again. The beauty of 'Evolution Rag' is that it is perfectly placed to fit in with the rest of the album: it's jolly but not silly, and while its vibe may run parallel to 'Waiting For You', it does it with a tad more substance. There's even a hint of a giggle in there: always a good sign in my book. Oh, and fans of Swanee-Kazoo on Radio Four will love it.

'Painted Chariot' (Heron)

Full-on rock mode, with (now) Fairport's Gerry Conway giving it some meat-and-two-veg drumming. It kicks off with Mike playing a riff of sorts on overdriven electric guitar, bass thunders along courtesy of Robin, and Malcolm plays mandolin. The lyrics are, once again, I believe, Scientology-driven. Though if you want to take them straight, as if buying a dodgy second-hand car, well, I guess that works too.

It all grinds along in fine fashion with Mike giving it his best rock voice until we hit a chanting section over the organ, and then it all goes bonkers. Mike thrashes out big electric chords over the organ, Robin does a big run down the bass, Gerry slips into Bonham mode, and it's a riffarama, as Mike picks up the beat, and somebody – I'm not sure who – brings in the horns on a countermelody. Is that what the ISB is now? Thrashing electric guitars and horn sections? Look, it all seemed very logical at the time and is perhaps even more so now: a band who had flourished with eclectic style and instrumentation, had no need to be demure about using what worked for a song. And here, they weren't. Of course, from here on in, it led to accusations that they were just browsing through style for the sake of it, but hadn't they always? Thus ended the vinyl side one.

Earlier on, I mentioned my forgotten Leeds encounter with Dr. Strangely Strange. This was the song that we sang and together. We might even have done Roy Harper's 'When An Old Cricketer Leaves The Crease'. Ah yes.

'Adam And Eve' (Williamson)

And as if to prove the point above, here Robin brings in ya reggae. Actually, there had been Caribbean influences in ISB songs from the start, so it was no great stylistic leap for this slight little song: replete with Malcolm doing a backing vocal in basso profondo, that always reminds me of The Spinners (the Liverpool ones with the kaftans, not the US soul ones). See the title? Yep, that's exactly what it's about: the bible story exactly as it is written, simple enough for a primary school sing-along.

Stan Lee makes his bass-playing debut, Mike hits the electric piano, Licky plays with her clashers (matron), and Malcolm plays a kind of calypso whistle riff, which reinforces my Spinners analogy. Robin contents himself on electric guitar: I wonder what they used? I've seen Fenders in live photos. Telecasters?

Just a thought. But it's a solid, if slight, song, which I often played during my busking days, much to the punters' generous delight (I wish).

'Red Hair' (Heron)

With this piece that Mike has returned to over the years, he presents such a heartfelt love song that it has to move the listener; at least the listener with a heart and soul. There's no huge overblown amour, just a simple love affair between two very normal people: not gods or mystical elves or the like. Mike's distinctive acoustic guitar alone more or less underpins the first verse before Robin's cello joins in. As an aside, Robin, for a while, featured a homemade electric cello on stage, which my reporter tells me was not the most musical of sounds. Anyway, here it's Robin on a standard cello. Its sliding notes echo his fiddle style – I have no doubt a classical player would, in the hearing, need to be carried out on a stretcher, but it works in its naivety. As the song builds, Mike adds piano and harmonium, and Licky plays pipe organ. There is a steady build to a crescendo, with the keyboards adding a mighty roar to the end. Perfect to my ears. As we shall see later, when they appeared post-ISB as a duo, Robin arranged it with Celtic harp. I now perform a hybrid version on my harp and love to play this beautiful song.

'Here Till Here Is There' (Williamson)

This is such a charming piece. Essentially unaccompanied, it is punctuated by a wind section of Robin and Malcolm's recorders and Mike on flute. It maintains the tradition of lyrics that appear to be non-specific but which hold meaning for the listener. Both Robin and Licky shine on the vocals here. There are hints of traditional music, but also simple art music too. The wind ensemble was a hardly-exploited area in the ISB canon, and as it works so well, you wonder why. Having Mike on flute is a rarity, and in Robin's philosophy, Mike doesn't do much with it, but what he does is perfect. The track also features a bass recorder for the only time on an ISB record. Again, it's a song I've performed, though only as a player, and I played the bass recorder part while my ex played tenor. Lovely. The song, not my ex.

'Tree' (Heron)

I assume Mike was looking back at what had gone before, as this is the first occasion where he revisited an older song (at least within the ISB studio recordings), in this case returning to a song from the very first album: which was only about five years previously, demonstrating how swiftly music moved in those days. You'll have to turn back a few pages to learn what the lyrics are about, so here we look at the musical arrangement. The whole thing has been strengthened, with Mike on piano and bouncy riffing between verses, with Malcolm's bouzouki and, primarily, Robin on mandolin. Does it add to the original? Well, both versions stand up in their own right, so it doesn't so much add as offer a complimentary second take. I would go for this version.

'Jigs: Eyes Like Leaves/Sunday Is My Wedding Day/Drops Of Whiskey/Grumbling Old Men' (Williamson / Trad. Arr. Williamson)

Although the jigs had left the recorded works early on (save for 'Fairies' Hornpipe' on *U*), they became a feature of the later stage show. Fairport Convention and Steeleye Span had proven them to be crowd-pleasers, provoking dancing outbreaks around the stage and twirling with abandoned enthusiasm, sometimes topless. And that was just the men. But here was a well-sorted folk rock set of tunes: namely, Robin's 'Eyes Like Leaves', coupled with the three traditional tunes, 'Sunday Is My Wedding Day', 'Drops Of Whiskey' and 'Grumbling Old Men'. Those readers of a musical bent can find the dots in Robin's book, *English, Welsh, Scottish and Irish Fiddle Tunes* (1976) (which comes with a CD of Robin playing tunes with Stan on bass. One for you completists). Robin's fiddle leads throughout in his own distinctive style, while Licky contributes spoons, autoharp and bodhran: here, curiously written as 'birrone'. Malcolm plays whistle and mandolin, and Mike bass. I bet this had them bouncing around. Later tunes wouldn't make the vinyl – 'Tear The Velvet' being one such – so it's actually rather nice to have this record of this aspect of the ISB.

'Darling Belle' (Williamson)

For many, this ranks high in Robin's list of most fully-realised songs. He has always said that this entire story came to him complete, in a dream. Robin seems adept at remembering dreams and creating songs from them. Rose mentions he did this a lot: an art I've never mastered.

Anyway, it's a story set in the period prior and moving into The Great War, or World War One. In the run-up to set the scene, we see a young schoolboy doing what young boys do: messing around in school, learning, and gaining amusement from passing wind. Meanwhile, a small girl feeds the swans in the park. She is a well-brought-up girl from a good family, as we can tell from the adept brush strokes mentioning the horses and referring to mother as 'mama'. Eventually, they meet – in (one presumes) late teenage years – and fall in love. They marry, but he goes to the front only two days after the ceremony and never returns. She spends her life mourning the loss.

So, a simple story that was probably played out across the world. But musically, Robin handles it with restraint and a sensible and apt use of instrumentation. Oh, and use of the voices. Licky, of course, plays the girl with a perfect voice that is at once warm and vulnerable. Robin is the young man (James) and avoids the vocal gymnastics, which wouldn't have added to the character. Malcolm also gets a lead vocal, forming a duologue with Robin. Mike adds backing vocals. The instrumental backing is always appropriate, gentle glockenspiel accentuating the period feel, for example. And during the interlude of 'Keep The Home Fires Burning', harmonica and clarinet capture the feel of the men singing together in the trenches. It's a lovely production, as voices cascade through the stereo, whispering, '...we regret to inform you...', and other sentences overlap in the sound, perfectly capturing those points of unbearable emotion where you don't listen but only hear, overwhelmed by the words inside your head.

If Island Records had had misgivings about their new signing, this track alone should have swept away their fears – as should much of this strong album, which took the band's past, retained the flavour, and updated. Things looked good.

Conclusion

In many respects, *Liquid Acrobat* was a return to form, though it has never been considered in the same esteem as those early Elektra albums. If some thought the band had strayed too far from base camp, many others realised that the patchouli oil and incense were drifting away in the breeze of the new decade, and the band had to move on.

Earthspan (1972)

Personnel:
Mike Heron: vocals, keyboards, acoustic and electric guitars, accordion
Robin Williamson: vocals, violin, cello, oboe, mandolin, bass guitar, Hardanger
fiddle, electric piano, viola, gimbri, Chinese flute, whistle
Licky McKechnie: vocals, bass guitar
Malcolm Le Maistre: vocals, acoustic guitar, mandolin, whistle, harmonium
With
Stuart Gordon: violin
Dave Mattacks: drums
Brian Davidson: drums
Jack Ingram: handclaps
Producer: Mike Heron and Robin Williamson
Record label: Island
Release date: November 1972
Chart position: UK: -, US: -
Running time: 41:11

I hope you're sitting down... *Earthspan* was the first String Band album that
I bought. I saw the band – this very line-up – at The Great Western Festival
near Lincoln (which is East – Yes, me neither) and loved them. More on that
encounter later. So when I saw this for sale on a stall in the old Bradford
Market, I snatched it up, natch. And I instantly loved it to bits. I had no
preconceptions for it to live up to, unlike some people, which is maybe why
so many dismiss the Island years: their heads are full of what went before. But
few bands stay the same, especially then, when a mixture of hard drugs, harder
business practices and social conditions dissipated the artistic propagation of
the late 1960s to early 1970s. Yes, the band were going into new areas – even
lounge jazz. But Robin was still scraping his gimbri, and Licky was still singing
clear as crystal. And although I'd heard them before at peoples 'pads', I didn't
have the weight of their history on my shoulders, so opening with one of
Malcolm's songs carried no major problems for me.

But here was the slickest album yet. Even from before dropping the needle
on the groove, you could tell by the cover: Mike looking cool in a blue
Kingfisher jacket. Lord, how I wanted a jacket like that, but never found one.
And hey, there's Mike again, looking all serious as he jots down the dots for a
proper musical arrangement. Malcolm looks all arty in half-light or walking up
a hillside in a loud tartan check jacket. Robin looks windswept and interesting
in sombre leisurewear. But Licky still looks cool, swinging on a swing, petting
a small bird or playing an old piano. But there were no bright dressing-up
clothes (well, apart from a bit of Malcolm), no garish sleeve. It was all very
stylish: We are serious musicians, we mean it, maaaan!

Inside, the music was a match. Gone were any stylistic traces of *Liquid
Acrobat* – things here flowed at an even pace. They functioned as a band.

No Licky bashing the drum kit; instead, seasoned session players. No Robin fiddling, but instead, real violin players. To some extent, the album was cohesive. Strange, because others don't agree; the opposite is also true.

The album title at least held onto the mystery of existence by using a line from 'Sunday Song', which was never used in the recorded version. Far out, man.

And the songwriting is shared here. Malcolm contributes strongly, as does Ms. McKechnie. Perhaps that alienated the *5000 Spirits* fans, but I loved the album, and truth be told, I still do.

'My Father Was A Lighthouse Keeper' (Le Maistre)

Malcolm is often cited as the beginning of the end for the band. But I think he was just caught in the moment of history that saw the steady splitting of two strong personalities. His songwriting was strong and certainly here on the opener: the first of his lighthouse songs. I believe the lighthouse keeper alludes to – again – religion. But if you want to cast that aside and take it as a literal reference, that works fine too.

Opening with a well-strummed acoustic, overlaid with a high violin figure, the song strides in in fine form, sounding perhaps more contemporary than the ISB had managed to before. There's even a reference to Coke cans! It all sounds like a band with somewhere to go, even if it was leaving behind where it had once been. The strings are fulsome and in a classical style. Any hint of enthusiastic amateurism had gone, forever. Mike had had his head down writing arrangements: the play-what-you-feel man had left the building.

'Antoine' (Heron)

Almost as a nod to earlier days, here is Mike solo. Well, the sole band member anyway – session musicians taking up the slack, again to add a more violinistic style that Robin's fiddling could not produce. That's not to belittle Robin's playing, but there is a marked difference between the two string-playing styles. Anyhoo, Mike plays a church organ – a real one by the sound of it – and sings of a French-sounding rural idyll: all walks to the church and love so pure. It is a beautiful song, and Mike sings it with a powerful yet restrained vocal. The late Stuart Gordon's strings complement the whole thing perfectly. Stuart was in a short-lived band called The Shortwave Band but found commercial success with The Korgis and their hit singles. He later worked with Steve Tilston before passing away a few years ago, far too early.

'Restless Night' (Williamson)

Enter young Robin, and here is the lounge jazz alluded to earlier. This is perhaps the largest style leap of all. There may have been country, ragtime, raga, Chinese influences and even trad jazz, but this was unexpected. It's 'No Sleep Blues' four years on, perhaps. Let's just say that again: four years. Most bands would spend that writing their next album, not moving steadily from that point to this point.

Above Robin's acoustic and Mike's electric piano were Mike's arranged horns, as per his cover photo. There are vague hints of changing melody lines, but it's nowhere near as marked as in the past. I keep using the word slick, but it's the only word for this. I actually like it, but probably in a way detached from the ISB – purely as a song and a performance. I get the impression that Robin was looking for his place in this new regime, trying on new suits to see how they looked. This one fitted well but was too tight around the elbows, perhaps.

'Sunday Song' (Heron/McKechnie)

At a little over seven minutes, this is the longest track on the album and perhaps the one with the best connection to what had gone before, with its constant changes throughout. Episodic may be the word. Licky wrote the lyrics and Mike wrote the music, and it's interesting how well the two seemed to work together on the few occasions this occurred.

Now, the lyrics. This is deep Scientology stuff, with the aliens setting up their secret settlements on Earth, hiding their wings away. You can't even look for a simpler explanation – this is hardcore. That said, I was able to listen and just enjoy the poetry of it all, long before I knew of the band's connection to Scientology. I just took it as a bit of cool sci-fi at the time.

Musically, it's beautifully-realised, both in composition and execution. Robin contributes oboe and mandolin, but this is largely Mike's creation. As far as I know, this was Licky's lyric and Mike's tune, though I'm thinking it was perhaps not so clear-cut, and involved a greater interplay between the two. The string arrangement is beautiful, with each taking separate roles: cello, viola and violins. And it all ends on a positive, repeated chorus, which is actually pretty uplifting. And thus ended the vinyl side one.

'Black Jack David' (Heron)

Mike again revisited what had gone before. Of note is the inclusion of two future members: Jack Ingram – on handclaps – who would later take the drum stool behind the band; and Stan Lee, who we have encountered before, on the bass. It's presumably by virtue of friendship that they are included: the band could surely have handled those duties in-house?

Although this is a great mid-album uplift and was no doubt a great stage favourite, it's hard to understand why it was included. Because Mike had no jolly songs in his head, perhaps? It is a good performance, but I'm not sure it really improves on the *I Looked Up* version. Maybe, they felt it would be a good taster for new fans and included it for those who would find *I Looked Up* to be hard going.

'Banks Of Sweet Italy' (Williamson)

I do love this song. It's almost a folk song in its construction, execution, and its tale of a sailor at sea missing his lover at home. It's a spit away from the many 'broken token' folk songs which abound in English folk music. And yet, the duologue between Robin's sailor and Licky's girl on shore – in 'red stockings and shoes of green' – is perfect. You can feel the longing and passion in their voices. Robin plays the Hardanger fiddle, which is a Norwegian variation with sympathetic strings beneath the fingerboard and a different tuning to the standard violin. If I was forced to pick a standout track from this album, this would be it. Robin was clinging to his folk roots; no matter where else, his muse was roaming.

'The Actor' (Williamson/Le Maistre)

More collaboration. Robin wrote the tune, and Malcolm the lyrics, which give a real feel for the 1920s artistic set, or perhaps how we think of those people of one hundred years ago: chaste love, where holding hands was daring enough. I tend to think, from other readings, that the creative set were at it like rabbits. But it doesn't take away from the gentle, wistful feel of Malcolm's words or Robin's perfectly-observed melody pastiche. I'm aware that many viewed 'The Actor' as anathema on an ISB album, but I still like it a lot, with its rippling guitar and a chorus that always sits on the brink of going into a jolly sing-along but holds back. For sure, Malcolm's rather cultured tones suit the vocals to a tee. In fact, his voice, in general, added another string to the ISB bow: Licky was very high, Robin was high, Mike was in the middle, while Malcolm added a deeper baritone to the sound. No wonder the likes of 'Here Till Here Is There' worked so very well. Divine, my dear, simply divine.

'Moon Hang Low' (Williamson)

If 'Restless Night' had flirted with lounge jazz, then here we have the full nine yards. Mike wrote the horn parts for the piece (so 'that's' what he's doing on the cover photo!), Robin contributing one of his more swooping vocals. He uses the techniques he truly began on *The Hangman's Beautiful Daughter* and applies them to jazz style, soaring hither and thither, spreading words over bar after bar, stretching the syllables as he goes. If you like this sort of thing, well, this will be to your liking. I've always placed it somewhere between 'It's fine, I can listen to it' and 'For Gawd's sake shift the needle!'. But in the end, does it work? Well, in the context of what it is, yes, it does. Would a real jazz afficionado agree? Well, perhaps not, but that's the ISB. A blues player wouldn't rate 'Robot Blues', a country player wouldn't rate 'Log Cabin Home In The Sky' etc.. But like Robin and instruments, it is what it is, and was not intended as a painstaking exploration of perfection.

'Sailor And The Dancer' (Le Maistre)

Malcolm's second solo songwriting credit is, strangely, perhaps the most ISB-like thing on the album: all mysterious lyrics regarding something mythical and involving a dancer – a theme which would pop up on his writing agenda time after time, even beyond the ISB. The tune is gentle and in keeping with what had gone before: Robin maintaining the spirit by adding gimbri and Chinese flute over Malcolm's harmonium. It would appear the band now had three songwriters and three vocalists. Hmm, is that too many? Not if they are all firing on all cylinders. Actually, there were four if you count Licky. Her 'Secret Temple' wasn't included on the album, but she was playing her part.

'Seagull' (Heron)

This track, with its rather strange musical structure, was my favourite on the album for a long time. As I understand, there was a Scientology ship where one went for enlightenment, and which was quite harsh on its students, and this song was Mike's end-of-term assessment of his visit, where it appears he didn't have too bad a time of it. Perhaps he was a good boy and avoided the rod of the cod-faced guru?

The song is based around electric guitar figures, including a solo that makes absolutely no sense at all, and yet, somehow, the opposite is also true, and it makes perfect sense – well, to me anyway. Then it suddenly explodes into a jolly rollicking sing-along at the end: 'Out on the rolling sea now'. Mike's on the accordion: another first (and last) for the band. It seemed things were going well for the revitalized rock version.

'Seagull' ended the album: a song that saw Licky play bass and make her last noises with the band, and saw Robin play the gimbri for the last time. Something was happening too: on the inner sleeve at the end was a picture of that nice geography teacher you used to like, and it said he was a new ISB member. What?

Conclusion

Earthspan is another of those albums that time has been kind to. It's a good set of songs and deserves its place in the ISB pantheon. 'Sunday Song', for example, showed an almost prog rock sensitivity, which hadn't been heard in ISB material before. *Tales of Gimbrigraphic Oceans*, anyone?

No Ruinous Feud (1973)

Personnel:
Mike Heron: bass guitar, guitars, keyboards, vocals
Malcolm Le Maistre: bass guitar, keyboards, vocals
Robin Williamson: fiddle, flute, guitars, keyboards, oboe, viola, whistle, vocals
Gerard Dott: woodwinds, keyboards
With
Alan Eden: drums
John Gilston: drums
Greyhound: Reggae band on 'Second Fiddle' (see text)
Jack Ingram: drums, guitar, percussion, vocals
Stan Lee: bass guitar, pedal steel guitar, vocals
Susie Watson Taylor: flute
Janet Williamson: flute
B. J. Wilson: drums
Producer: Roger Mayer and Mike Heron
Record label: Island
Release date: March 1973
Chart position: UK: -, US: -
Running time: 38:42

Oh, how things had changed and yet remained the same. After having first appeared on *5000 Spirits*, Licky had gone, after a run exceeded only by Robin and Mike. As I recall at the time, it was said she was taking a sabbatical and would return after a while. She never did. And, sadly, nobody is really sure what became of her. Rumours abound: she was last seen walking into the desert; she had learned dark secrets about the Scientology organization and had to hide away as they were after her; or she just got tired of the music business and hid herself. Rose' view is that Licky has passed away. There are unclaimed royalties, and Licky was together enough to have claimed some at some point. Maybe we will never know, or maybe someday, maybe, we will find out the full story.

But meanwhile, who was that masked geography teacher we saw on the *Earthspan* sleeve insert? Well, he was/is Gerard Dott: Lickys replacement, coming in on clarinet, sax and keyboards, playing ragtime in concert. He had known Mike since school days and was an accomplished musician who worked in a music store while playing in jazz bands. How this all got him into the ISB is anybody's guess, really. A grasp at a new sound using the instruments that even Robin hadn't played, perhaps? Gerard certainly wasn't in any way a direct replacement for Licky's vocals and bass and so on. In any case, his tenure was short-lived, being less than a year. He was the only non-Scientologist in the band, which may have had a bearing on things. At any rate, he was politely asked to leave. But he made it onto one album, and this is it.

Well, I might as well come right out and say it: ask any String-head what the worst album they ever made was, and this will inevitably be it. The shock began with the cover: four smooth head-and-shoulder shots of the band all wearing cool gear. Well, cool for 1973, and I think we all know what that means. Yep, Malc in a huge red tartan check jacket, Mike in a suit and tie (!), Gerard all brown suede and velvet with hat covering his receding hairline, and Robin in a big old white gipsy-style shirt. And the photographs were only taken by David bloody Bailey! And in the middle, a horrific pastel-shade pop-art explosion graphic with the album title and band name in the middle. It didn't bode well. The rear just had the song titles. I believe the details were on an insert, though personally, I've never seen one.

So, is it as bad as they all say? Well, actually, perhaps not. Taken a track at a time, there are some gems here, but as a whole, there is filler, and there are at least two absolute clunkers. It wasn't even all original material. It's reported that around this time, the band was following the path to rock/pop status: afore long, teenage girls would invade the stage, leaving Robin bemused and unhappy. The cracks were showing. Best then to take this one step at a time.

'The Explorer' (Heron)

Opening in a bevvy of flutes here was at least one link with the past: the girlfriends. Not Rose and Licky, but Janet Williamson nee Shankman, and Susie Watson-Taylor: Mike's then girlfriend and manager of the band. At this point, it's probably best not mention Janine (a *This Is Spinal Tap* reference, for those not in the know). Maybe they did design costumes based on their star signs. In Dolby.

Although 'The Explorer' is actually a pretty good example of pop/rock – and would have slid effortlessly into Mikes post-ISB solo work – it must still have been something of a shock to the fans brought up on patchouli oil and Afghan coats. The lyrics relate a tale of a lost explorer: no mystic references, just a straight-ahead story. As I say, it's actually a pretty neat bit of work, with a real bass and drums setup. There are a few drummers on the album, including Alan Eden, who had been with the seminal and distinctly left-field folk rock band, Mr Fox. I once interviewed Alan. It was a great chat that ended in a competition to work out who was the strangest person we'd ever played with. Alan won. But I digress. As an opener, 'The Explorer' sent out a clear signal: the band was either on a path to destruction or to greater public aplomb in the wider world of entertainment. For the fans, there was trepidation as to which.

'Down Before Cathay' (Le Maistre)

Once again, there was Malcolm keeping some of the old magic going, with tales of old, mystic intimations, and a more acoustic approach. Some years after the band split, Malcolm was at the ISB convention that took place in Hebden Bridge, and performed this song amongst the new songs from his solo album, *Nothing Strange*. The song had aged well – if it had aged at all – and proved its worth as a composition.

As I said in the introduction, there are gems on this least-regarded ISB album, and this is one of them. The album credits always seemed haphazard: there seems to be a concertina – featuring heavily here – for which nobody is credited. It could be Robin, but of his many instruments, the concertina is not noted, the nearest being his occasional use of piano accordion. Was it a session player? Jack Emblow perhaps? Maybe even Alistair Anderson who I saw play with Robin once? Is it an emulatingkeyboard. My musician's ear says not. Either way, it's a great little embellishment, that adds to the sailor feel of the piece (even though the concertina didn't appear until long after the days of sailing ships, no matter what Hollywood tells you!).

'Saturday Maybe' (Williamson)

As Robin enters the writing credits, it's a shock to find it is with a beautifully observed song about a mundane and illicit love affair. No coal is shovelled, no ducks are on ponds, just factory smoke and electric fires, as the lover awaits the husband's departure to the pub before entering to an electric fire and a green slip dropping to the floor. And not even her tears are allowed as it may 'freak the baby'. In fact, that's the only line that jars modern ears with its dated style.

The tune reflects the yearning perfectly: the sense of hopelessness in not knowing when they can next grab their precious time together. It really is a wonderful piece of work and follows a line that would largely be abandoned in Robin's writing after the ISB. What do they mean this is a terrible album? To my mind, it would happily share a room with 'The Queen of Love' as a counterpoint. That's three good songs in a row!

'Jigs' (Trad. Arr. Williamson)

Again, a set of traditional tunes led by Robin's fiddle, which are neither mundane nor set the world alight – they just form a pleasant interlude. It's back to the way of the first album jigs. Jack Ingram plays the electric guitar here, I believe: again, quite why, when given the three guitarists in the band, I can't say. One little clunker, though: the rather weak title of 'Jigs' was made ludicrous by the extra album sleeve subtext describing them as a 'selection of traditional reels'. Now, for the non-musical, a jig is a jig and a reel is a reel. It's down to time signature and structure. The description was like calling your meal a T-Bone steak and then adding it will consist of a selection of vegeburgers.

Anyway, debate sometimes flares up as to what the tunes are. But to my ear, the main one is 'Speed The Plough', though in its slightly more Americanised form, which has a different title. Either way, it's not a patch on the *Liquid Acrobat* tune set.

'Old Buccaneer' (Williamson)

And here's where it gets messy, with the first of two Robin songs that produce snorts of horror and derision from aficionados. I mean, for all its jaunty tune and Scooby Doo spooky bits, Enid Blyton could have written the storyline for *The Famous Five*: kids find old man smoking fags and drinking rum, and befriend him. Yeah, I know, these days you'd be speed-dialling Social Services, what with him lighting the kids ciggies and all, but here he's just an old chap telling them what he got up to on the rolling, rolling sea. You get the feeling Robin was grasping for a commercial direction to match with Mike and came up with this. Actually, there's worse to come, but there you go. Funnily enough, I am told on reliable authority from a man in the know that by 2019, Robin had started performing the song in his solo set. I'd like to hear it – see if there's a pearl in that shell. At any rate, it gave Gerard a workout on his woodwind section, so…

'At The Lighthouse Dance' (Le Maistre)

Look, it's a really cool riff. I mean, okay, riffing isn't necessarily the first thing that springs to mind when you think ISB, but it is cool. And I've always held a great affection for this song. The lyrics – and this from Malcolm's lips – concern the band happening to be in Ulverston on the edge of the lake district while touring. Ulverston isn't coastal, but the lighthouse refers to the Sir John Barrow Monument, which stands atop a hill to the edge of the town, and is – to all intent and purposes – a lighthouse in design. Anyhoo, Malcolm went to a local dance in town, where a local band was playing, and, well, that's about it really, except for a middle bit with space invaders and masqueraders present. But it certainly is a 'bopping' number – to use 1970s jargon – and is, for me, very endearing in its standard band instrumentation. I perhaps hold it in affection because, as a callow teen, I encountered a local rock band playing on a temporary bandstand in Ulverston during a town festival. I heard their guitars and I saw girls looking at them, and at that moment, my future life was set out before me. So thank you, Malcolm. End of vinyl side one.

'Second Fiddle' (Duke Reid)

Here is Robin and Gerard in perfect unison on whistle and clarinet, backed by the reggae band, Greyhound. What?? Now, I'm happy to be corrected on the reasons for this, but insider info tells me Island Records had this idea that they would create a one-off album that would pair some of their white artists with their black reggae artists. It faltered and never got off the ground, but this was one of the tracks that did get made. I believe John Martyn with Johnny Too Bad was the only other released example. To tantalize you, it's said that Jethro Tull and Bob Marley and the Wailers would have been paired too. I mean, that sounds interesting, and certainly, this little instrumental is a bit of commercial reggae with glorious playing from the ISB lads, and it's tantalizing as to what the entire album could have sounded like. Imagine the Wailers covering 'Waltz Of The New Moon': that would have been so much more interesting! Finally, in case you were wondering, this tune was originally done by Tommy McCook and the Supersonics in 1968. You're welcome.

'Circus Girl' (Williamson)

I said in the introduction that this was the ISB album least-regarded by fans, and here we have the album's least-regarded track. Yes, it's that weak. It aims for the charm and gentle humour of the past but slips and falls on its face. You know when your mate tells you a joke that you've heard before, and you have to fake laughing? It's a little like that. Well, yes, I did see them perform it live, and as an amusing few minutes in a concert, it just squeezed by. But this silly tale of love for a circus girl does nobody any favours and would've been best left to the likes of the stage-only material like 'Giles The Crocodile': 'You had to be there', never rung so true. But again, it was a chance for Gerard to display his talents, it's only two and a half minutes long, and you do get that circus tune we all know so well. So, well, there I've ended on a positive. Just.

'Turquoise Blue' (Heron)

In a wash of acoustic guitars and soft wind instruments, this gentle little bossa nova love song lifts the album, and once more, you can hear this in Mike's post-ISB songs. It's nothing earth-shattering, but a lovely bit of singing and playing. Little more can be said.

'My Blue Tears' (Dolly Parton)

At this stage, outside of country music circles – in Britain at least – Dolly Parton was not a known quantity. Which of the band decided to cover the song is not known, though usually, Malcolm gets the credit as he is the lead vocalist here. At two minutes, it doesn't outstay its welcome, and it has to be said that Gerard shines here with a blistering clarinet arrangement that blasts the song along. If you visit YouTube, you can find many versions of the song; but actually, this must rank as one of the best beyond Ms. Parton's own version. No, really. Why it's on an ISB album? Well, that's more open to debate, I suspect.

'Weather The Storm' (Williamson)

There's little to truly dislike about this straight-ahead bit of sing-along candy floss from Robin, except that it 'is' Robin: you just expected better. Musically, it fires along okay – all band members giving it their professional all – but it's just a 'happy-song-by-numbers' affair. I wish I could say more, but it borrows phrases from other songs and has little substance. Sad.

'Little Girl' (Heron)

The album ends with gently acoustic romantics from Mike. It's a sweet, gentle number, but a strange way to end the album. For all its faults, 'Weather The Storm' could have been a better finisher.

Conclusion

And thus ended an album that aimed for a new direction, but kept hitting walls. It's telling that even the title was chosen as the best of a bad bunch, according to Gerard. They'd looked for a corporate link between Mike and Robin and just widened the chasm. Or so it seemed.

Funny: when our band, The Glad Undertakers, was looking at which ISB songs to cover, we were all surprised how often numbers from this album came to mind. So maybe it had some merit, was just of its time, and too much of a leap from what had gone before.

Hard Rope & Silken Twine (1974)

Personnel:
Robin Williamson: guitars, whistle, congas, fiddle, flute, oud
Mike Heron: Guitars, keyboards, sitar, vocals
Malcolm Le Maistre: Vocals
Graham Forbes: Guitars
Jack Ingram: Drums
Stan Lee: Bass guitar, lap steel guitar
Producer: Mike Heron
Record label: Island
Release date: March 1974
Chart position: UK: 203, US: -
Running time: 43:51

The frustrating thing about this final album, is that it's actually very good, and seemed to have resolved the last album's issues. The cover was a nice painting of natural things and fairy folk – by Wayne Anderson whose work graced many fantasy and children's books – and it was classy, where the *No Ruinous Feud* cover was just out of alignment with the band. And a band they now were: a rock band, with little to be heard in the way of esoteric instrumentation: just a flash of Mike's sitar and Robin's oud. The rats had long ago eaten the gimbri (no, really, according to Robin).

It's frustrating that this was where it all ended, because there seemed to be a strong route ahead. But the only glimpse we have of that route, are a couple of tracks that surfaced on Mike's post-ISB album, *Reputation*: recorded for Melanie's Neighbourhood Records label, where the ISB would have been heading after their Island contract ended. There's also a couple of songs that have subsequently appeared that show the potential next album could have been a pretty good affair. But that is the speculative. Here we are now with this album, which ended the saga, at least as far as studio albums as The Incredible String Band go. See later chapters for further information.

Hard Rope & Silken Twine was an album of two vinyl sides: side one was songs by the three writers – with barely a bad track there – while side two was a complete Mike Heron piece called 'Ithkos', made up of various sections. Here was a band seemingly working together: Mike and Robin once again individual and collective on each other's works, and Malcolm now the singer and – in live performance – the showman. And to beef it up, Jack Ingram was given membership status on the drums, and Stan the bass duties too. On the electric guitar was Scottish rock plank-spanker Graham Forbes (all-'round lovely bloke, and author of a number of highly-readable books, two of which are autobiographical and feature background to this era of the band).

I saw this version of the band on stage and they really were great. They functioned as a tight band, with the occasional return to the duo format and even the theatrics of *U*, with the saga of 'Giles The Crocodile' allowing Malcolm to dress up and prance around the stage to his heart's content. This album may not quite reach the joy of those live shows, but it's still a solid album and a logical development from what had begun less than ten years before. Those who wish to see the band in action, can refer to a film called *Rehearsal*, which features a few musical units, errr, rehearsing. See 'Ithkos' below for more details.

'Maker Of Islands' (Heron)
If you want an example of how the band had moved along, the truly superb opener shows that already-good songs like 'Little Girl' could have been better had the same level of attention been applied. The arrangement is superb, with a perfect string section blending with Mike's yearning vocals: the lyrics looking for real love beyond the one-night stand. It's always a good yardstick when the length of a song is just right. This never seems to be six minutes long: it feels about four because each part of it is right. It's so good, that even I covered it! So, was this the way things might have gone? – beautifully put together soft rock? Perhaps. 'Evie' and 'Meanwhile The Rain' – which we shall talk about later – said yes. But all such from Mike: would Robin have settled into that? We will never really know.

'Cold February' (Williamson)
There must have been a collective sigh of relief when this song appeared on vinyl. Gone was Robin's dalliance with rock and pop. Here were the Scottish roots showing through, with a simple arrangement of Mike on organ and Robin on vocals and whistle, taking you back to those heady *Hangman* days. Robin's voice just soars and shows just the right level of emotion. It was recorded live: one of two tracks here to never get a studio release. No matter, its simplicity hints that it wouldn't be bettered in the studio.

The lyric laments the stupidity of war and the damage it causes. Initially, Robin had written the lyrics to specifically refer to the troubles in Ulster but then cut back to a more general statement. Given the IRA's reputation at the time, that may have been a wise move. But this doesn't detract from the overall power of the song. Live, tingles went down my spine.

'Glancing Love' (Le Maistre/Gilston)
Malcolm's songwriting was getting stronger, and here, let me once again recommend his post-ISB solo album, *Nothing Strange*. Right, that done, here is a tale of boyhood fervour for a star of the silver screen. That seems to be the case, and I have no reason to doubt it. Malcolm certainly had moved on from the hippie sagas that had been his forte. It's a slick piece of soft rock and may not be groundbreaking, but it's most enjoyable and is enhanced by Robin's only known outing on the alto flute: a deeper-toned variant of the usual concert flute. As a writer, I think you tend to write according to your circumstances. There's no point writing for a full symphony orchestra

when all you have to work with is an acoustic guitar and a school keyboard. Thus, I perhaps feel Malcolm's writing here is influenced by the band of solid musicians around him. Glen Row was both home and rehearsal space, so developing an idea was not out of the question.

'Dreams Of No Return' (Williamson)

Robin was certainly firing on all cylinders, with a song that not only links the ISB's legacy of tempo and melody changes with Mike's final sitar outing but moves them into a new era. His playing is exemplary here, superb picked guitar in total harmony with the sitar. The words are poetic again – no circus girls here – and perhaps mean what you want them to mean. There's a slowing of tempo, as Robin and Mike play in unison before a sitar/guitar call-and-response, then into a lifting, faster end section. Fabulous. Fabulous and overlooked. This perfect blend of legacy and future, offered so much promise.

'Dumb Kate' (Heron)

If there's a clunker on the album, then I suppose this is it. Though, to be fair, this hangs mainly on the lyrics, which even at the time, smacked of male chauvinism. This would be, I suspect, an attempt to have another jolly stomp-along in the way of 'Log Cabin Home In The Sky' or 'Black Jack David' (which sat alongside it in the live repertoire). Robin plays his scratchy-style fiddle over a fairly lacklustre bass-led backing, with Robin and Mike singing in unison through much of the song. It's another live take of a song that never had a studio version: in a way, a shame. With good production and changed lyrics, it could have worked pretty well, I reckon. As it is, well, nice try but no cigar.

'Ithkos' (Heron with contributions from Graham Forbes and Robin Williamson)

Before we start, I best list the individual sections of Mike's near-20-minute piece. Sardis (Oud Tune), Lesbos: Dawn, Lesbos: Evening, Aegean Sea, Dreams Fade, Port Of Sybaris, Go Down Sybaris, Huntress, Hold My Gaze.

Robin composed the opening instrumental, Sardis, and played the oud: again a link to as far back as *5000 Spirits* and the trip to Morocco. There's also a rather splendid electric violin solo from Robin. The main thing that hits you is that here – perhaps for the only time on the album – the band are playing as a band, with Graham Forbes, in particular, shining with some strident yet restrained electric guitar. I understand he also composed some of the melody lines contained therein. Malcolm takes the lead vocals for much of the piece.

But if you really want to know how this piece was put together, behold, you can! A director called James Archibald produced a film called *Rehearsal*, which did pretty much what it said on the tin. Four groups of musicians were chosen to be in the film, and we watched all go from conception to performance. The ISB were the choice for the rock element, and the fly on the wall sees the band at their Glen Row cottages, putting 'Ithkos' together.

If nothing else, it shows the cracks: Mike berating drummer Jack Ingram, Robin looking a little bored and sidelined to the role of backing musician. Despite the concept, only the ISB were shown in the final performance (for cost reasons) and can be seen performing 'Ithkos' at the Colston Hall, Bristol, in October 1973 (before the name change from Colston, obviously). Anyway, you'll find it on YouTube if you want to see for yourself. It's an entertaining watch, sometimes unwittingly funny – for example, Malcolm with headphones on rehearsing his vocals. A man sat in a cottage, periodically shouting 'Ithkos', cannot help but raise a smile.

But back to the record. I've been listening to it since I bought the album on its day of release all those years ago, and I still couldn't truly tell you what the story is about, and yet it doesn't matter to me because it's a beautifully executed work.

Conclusion

And it's the last notes of music you would hear from the String Band, or at least the original version of a band that had lasted less than ten years; a band whose fortunes had risen and fallen (the album peaked at 203 in the charts, helping along the demise), and whose influence would grow and grow after they had gone. They survived the punk put-downs of all things hippie to suddenly emerge as a seminal influence on many musicians: Robert Plant and Kate Bush being just two such. As the CD years entered and the back catalogue became more readily available, the Elektra re-releases became the label's best sellers: outselling even The Doors. But more of that later. For now, a curtain had come down.

It's hard to gauge the reaction at the time. Remember, the days of social media were many years in the future, so earnest lamentations that a band had split were limited to the inky weekly music papers and their letters pages. I was certainly sad to see them go, but there was so much good music around (or is that just my rose-tinted specs?), that I don't remember locking myself in my room for months. *No Ruinous Feud* had diminished the band's standing, so I suspect many simply clung to the early albums, having slowly drifted from the concert halls, albeit replaced by some younger fans. All things must pass. And they had. Was it forever? Maybe someday...

Smiling Men With Bad Reputations and Myrrh

Although both the leading members of the band have released numerous albums since 1974, those largely lie outside the scope of this book, our concern here being the band as a band. Some of the post-1974 work will be mentioned briefly in a later chapter. But two solo albums that do need to be looked at are those produced while the ISB was still a going concern, not least because some of their songs found their way into the ISB live repertoire. They also make an interesting case study. It's simplistic to say that Mike's is the rock album, and Robin's the esoteric world music acoustic album, as close inspection shows that to be only partially true. Robin rocks along nicely on 'Sandy Land', and Mike couldn't be more String than on 'Spirit Beautiful'.

According to Mike, the rockier songs on *Smiling Men With Bad Reputations* were written while staying with friends in America: they created their own very strong coffee, and as a result, Mike was speeding, making it the only known album where the drug of choice was caffeine.

The covers, of course, don't help to dispel these views. Robin stands on a hillside near Glen Row, in ethnic garb, making strange hand signals to a bunch of similarly-clad 'heads', including Malcolm, Licky, and the dog, Leaf. Mike stands in a silver foil room, surrounded by primary colours, holding out a pineapple to all manner of characters from around the world, as comic book speech bubbles emanate from the chaps. And yet, they are two sides of the same coin: both show the musician standing apart from the crowd and gesturing a message of sorts. I mean, wasn't the gods scene in the *Be Glad* film, heavy on the tin foil too?

For sure, Robin's is the harder album, though like any music, it's worth the effort in the end. But Mike's album – despite having commercial-sounding tracks – can be equally challenging. You can read what you will into the fact that Mike's album was on the Island label, while Robin's was on an Island offshoot called Help (where all albums were around a quid cheaper than a normal release). Maybe Robin was wanting to make things easier on the pockets of his audience? Or maybe Island simply didn't think that the commercial prospects were high, so helped his album along with a budget release. Who knows. We do know that here were two fine albums that both deserve a place here.

Smiling Men With Bad Reputations – Mike Heron (1971)
Personnel:
Mike Heron: guitars, keyboards, sitar, harmonica, vocals
With
John Cale: bass guitar, guitar, harmonium, piano, viola, vocals
Gerry Conway: drums
Tony Cox: VCS3 synthesizer
Pat Donaldson: bass guitar
Dr. Strangely Strange: backing vocals

Ronnie Lane: bass guitar
Sue Glover and Sunny Leslie (Often referred to as Sunny and Sue): backing vocals
Mike Kowalski: drums
Dave Mattacks: drums
Keith Moon: drums
Simon Nicol: guitar
Dave Pegg: bass guitar
Dudu Puckwana: sax and piano
Rose Simpson: bass guitar
Liza Strike: backing vocals
Richard Thompson: guitar
Pete Townshend: guitar
Heather Wood: vocals
Producer: Joe Boyd
Record label: Island (UK), Elektra (US)
Release date: 30 April 1971
Running time: 45:39

'Call Me Diamond' (Heron)
And straight into a track that declared, this isn't the String Band. It's a lightly world-flavoured tune, sprinkled with a strong rhythm section, including Simon Nicol: the latest of the Fairport Convention recruits from the Witchseason stable, to play on ISB-related sessions. Add to that the sunshine of Dudu Pukwana's sax, and you have a mighty opener that sets out the album's intent. I mean, for goodness sake, it's catchy, it rocks along in a way that those so-inclined could cut a rug to, and Mike doesn't hold back on the vocal front. Sure, lines like 'Kiss me all along my spine' were not your average top ten lyrics, and there was probably more hidden meanings in there, but who's nit-picking? It was a breathtaking opener.

'Flowers Of The Forest' (Heron)
One of the songs not from the coffee rush, taking its title from a Scottish folk song that Scottish military pipe bands sometimes played as an instrumental lament. The title is all that Mike borrowed unless you include the mighty Richard Thompson, who contributes some wonderful lead guitar to the piece (incidentally, he played the Scottish folk song of the same name on Fairport's *Full House* album), blending effortlessly with Mike's chorded acoustic and Rose Simpson's incredible (sic) bass guitar-playing. If she says she only did as she was told, here is the proof that her soul seeped through into her fingers. Shame then that this was her finale on record: she left the ISB soon after the sessions. When I last interviewed Rose, this was one of the tracks she chose to bookend the radio interview. There's nothing mystical in the lyrics. It's a straight love song, but beautiful too.

'Audrey' (Heron)

The love songs continue with this lovely song, which does work in two separate parts, as ISB tradition dictates. It features John Cale heavily on keyboards as he was over in Europe. (Although from Wales, he was living in America, coming to fame as a member of The Velvet Underground, sawing away at a viola in a way his classical training may not have prepared the world for. While here, may I recommend his album, *Paris 1919*. It's one of his finest.)

The initial part of the song sees Mike singing over a repeated descending harpsichord riff. Of note, for me at any rate, is the line, 'Tonight won't you come and make love to me', which, after years of pop, we know is the socially acceptable form of a pastime beginning with the letter F. But here, it really does sound sexual. Anyway, there's a cross-fade as the harpsichord drifts off and the harmonium drifts in, the final verses passing by as the romance unfolds. On first hearing, I was confused but interested enough to persevere, and the reward was hearing what a brilliant track it was. Is Audrey a real woman, a pseudonym for a real woman, or simply an invention?

'Brindaban' (Heron)

The title? I'm glad you asked. It's the name of the village that Krishna called home. And the peacocks etc.? They are the mnemonics for notes in an Indian music scale. Whether this adds up to a deep and meaningful revelation or just interesting words is probably up to you. But what is of chief note here is the excellent woodwind arrangement provided by one Gerard Dott, making this his first ISB-linked appearance: no doubt we thought little of it at the time, but in retrospect, here was the start.

Musically, it is a bit of joy, though often overlooked among the more 'heavy' items here on the menu. But it is lovely and again indicates future ISB paths. It also illustrates that Scientology hadn't totally taken away Heron's ability to consider other philosophies within the songs.

'Feast Of Stephen' (Heron)

The original side one's closer was a bit of a stunner and has remained in the Heron live repertoire for many years. Mike would say that he had the idea of writing the verses for Christmas cards and earning some money from that and that this was his idea. Well, I'm not sure, but it's certainly a great uplifting song. The arrangement is pretty much down to John Cale, who told Mike he'd written too many chords, then made it simpler, playing the majority of the track's instruments. Just when Mike sings about the fiddler, Cale comes in on viola. Now, as a musician, this sticks in my craw, but it's a trivial wee thing.

The song states its first verse twice, the second time adding to the arrangement. There's a melancholy middle-eight, before an extended coda with a nod to The Beatles' 'Hey Jude', as Mike sings 'My love' with gusto, and the session girls don't go 'doo dah doo', but reply with 'fly she flies' – as uplifting an experience as you could wish for. Thank goodness it didn't end up on the inside of a piece of paper with a jolly robin on the front. Now that would have been ironic!

'Spirit Beautiful' (Heron)
If there's a track on the album that would get the prize for 'most stringy song', this is it. Indeed, it can be found on live ISB recordings from the time. It's all Indian instruments and melody, the instruments being from members of the local Indian community. Dr. Strangely Strange (see *Myrrh* for more Strangely influences) and Heather Wood share the backing vocals. Heather was a member of the influential folk trio, The Young Tradition, which also included Royston Wood (no relation) and my late friend, Peter Bellamy.

The lyrics explore inner growth: pebbles become mountains, streams become oceans, and so on. It's a mesmerizing piece of work, which Mike was still being performing in the 21st century – though, sadly, not on sitar. When last I saw the song performed, a stick dulcimer was employed for the sitar part.

'Warm Heart Pastry' (Heron)
And back to the coffee-fueled songs and riffarama. Also, welcome as the backing band, Tommy and the Bijoux! Well, actually, some of The Who – Pete Townshend and Keith Moon – with Ronnie Lane of The (Small) Faces on bass. Accounts relate a good deal of drinking on the sessions, while Joe Boyd tells how Pete worked the song up from Mike's little idea into the quite Who-like beast that resides here. If anyone didn't know it was Pete and Keith, the playing would instantly tell you: nobody drums like my late namesake, and nobody thrashes power chords like Pete. John Cale drops in some quite eerie viola, though it appears to be an overdub: the lightweight Cale having not made it out of the pub in time to play live.

I think this has to stand as the track that most separates Mike from the ISB of the time, as well as point – in a more extreme way – in the direction the band would slowly take before they split. By the way, history does not relate just how The Who got involved here. Even Pete's autobiography, while mentioning the session, does not say how it all came about. Anyway, let's raaaaaaaaawk! (Puts up first finger and pinky and nods head vigorously.)

'Beautiful Stranger' (Heron)
The synthesizer was just there, having become part of modern music. But back at this time, the player credit – in this case, Tony Cox (not the one once married to Yoko Ono) – was accompanied by the make of synth. Here it's an EMS VCS 3. Elsewhere, Moogs and Wasps etc., would all be namechecked until everything just became a synth.

The track opens with the synth's swooping burbles, creating a texture hardly heard back then. Mike plays electric guitar with no effects, just the straight, brittle sound of a solid guitar through a decent amp, alongside a heartfelt vocal. Again, the use of the electric is unusual, along a line that once would have been acoustic territory. It's all gentle and mysterious intimations of the Westerner in an exotic third-world location until it suddenly kicks into a rocky chorus, replete with drums, bass and female backing vocals behind Mike's suddenly raucous vocal. Yes, the shift does reflect the age-old ISB trick, but it is a pretty nice bit of work and does create a bridge from 'Warm Heart Pastry' to the closing track.

'No Turning Back' (Heron)
Finishing on such a tender acoustic solo piece may seem strange. Again, the lyrics are ambiguous: is it aimed at a lover or the singer's son? It's probably not of great import for the overall feel of the song – in fact, it probably adds to the atmosphere. Totally gorgeous, the song ends with the acoustic guitar's dying note. What an album!

'Make No Mistake' (Heron)
There was also a single issued, of which this was the B-side. This and the next track were added to the 2005 CD remaster: prior to which release, grown men would sell their own children to obtain a copy. And probably did. I travelled to the leafy suburbs of South London to hear it in the abode of a man who actually owned a copy, along with Vashti Bunyan's album. This is a jolly little piece that rocks along nicely, Mike giving it some harmonica. A special note must be given to the pianist: a bloke from Pinner called Reg Dwight, though perhaps better-known as Elton John. On the cusp of his rise to stardom, he was keeping the wolf from the door with session work, and if you can find it, there is a demo album known as *The Saturday Sun Sessions*. This was put together at Joe Boyd's behest to showcase the Witchseason Productions' songwriters in an attempt to get their songs covered. There are tracks written by Nick Drake and others, including Mike Heron, who is represented by 'This Moment'. The female vocalist is Linda Peters, also to find great fame later, by her married name of Linda Thompson: wife of Richard.

'Lady Wonder' (Heron)
The single's A-side was quite a commercial piece of pop/rock, again, chiefly given credence by the electric guitar player on it, who was that there Jimmy Page of rock giants, Led Zeppelin. This is the reason the single became doubly collectable after its deletion. Those Zep and ISB completists all wanted a copy, as would a collector of Island singles, no doubt. It's a good-enough song, but I suspect much of the legend lay in its lack of availability. The same applied to Vashti Bunyan's *Just Another Diamond Day* album, now readily available on CD, following a bout of interest after the title track was used in a TV advert. I mention it here, as Mike and Robin both appear on that album.

Conclusion

The changes that *Smiling Men With Bad Reputations* saw were marked: Mike not even being instrumentally credited (you have to work it out from what you can hear that's not credited to anyone else), and yet, maybe we knew what was going on. 'Red Hair' and 'Painted Chariot' could have changed places with tracks here without any real problem. Meanwhile, back at Glen Row...

Myrrh – Robin Williamson (1972)

Personnel:
Robin Williamson: vocals, guitars, oboe, jews harp, gong, bouzouki, cello, bombarde, violin, piano, bass guitar, flute, mandolin
With
Janet Williamson: organ, piano
Stan Lee Buttons: organ, pedal steel guitar, bass guitar
Susie Watson-Taylor: flute
David Campbell: viola
Gerry Conway: drums
Producer: Roger Mayer, Stan Schnier and Robin Williamson
Record label: Edsel
Release date: 1972
Running time: 39:16

Here was a different kettle of fish: much more acoustic, though not wholly so and much more challenging. It was altogether more String Band than *Smiling Men*, though it had more the older sound than what the band was becoming. It's an album that repays repeated listening to fully appreciate its nuance and complexity, but in the end, it's worth the effort. Incidentally, the afore-mentioned cover is telling you things within the people's hand gestures and reproduction of Egyptian hieroglyphics: so now you know.

'Strings In The Earth And Air' (Ivan Pawle and James Joyce)

Opening with the album's only non-original, here is the Dr. Strangely Strange connection, with Ivan Pawle's concoction of his music and a couple of James Joyce poems. The backing is primarily string quartet, flutes adding texture hither and thither, and the subtlest of bass guitar. It's an opener that sets the tone of the album: a cold but friendly landscape to wander through.

'Rends-Moi Demain' (Williamson)

Much of the album is based around love songs, and what's the most romantic of languages? Well, it's perhaps debatable, but I'd go for French. And so would Robin, as this totally entrancing love song proves. At this point, Robin and Janet's relationship was quite new, was quite new, though it underpinned the album. It's a simple arrangement here: Robin's fingerpicked acoustic made the smoother by Stan's pedal steel. If you're wondering why Stan has a slightly different name here, it's because he had no UK work permit. He is actually called Stan Schnier. But that's an aside.

Robin, at his most romantic, is as romantic as you need. There's a clip of the ISB from a French TV show, where he is interviewed and speaks in French throughout. How well, I couldn't say, but who knew?

'The Dancing Of The Lord Of Weir' (Williamson)

On those long-ago computer night shifts, this was the track that caused my fellow workers to threaten me with violence if I didn't lift the needle off the record. I can kind of see their point, much as I enjoy the track. It's almost like Robin is trying to reinvent music and throw out most of what went before. A strummed bouzouki underpins, its open strings ringing out in a high-pitched drone, the beat and tempo of the instrument varying to fit in with the song's lines. Elsewhere, gongs, percussion and bombarde, increase the feeling that you've fallen through into another dimension.

Lyrically, it's a fairly standard folk tale: peaceful, creative people are attacked by heathen hoards, who kidnap the lovely young girl and sweep her off to the castle. The villagers form a band (natch!) and, in disguise, visit the castle to offer up a free gig. But magic is afoot, and as soon as the baddies start dancing, they can never stop, so the nice ones get the girl and go home happily. Oh, and Robin's vocals are off the scale here.

'Will We Open The Heavens' (Williamson)

Robins deft acoustic guitar is to the fore again in this love song, along with flutes aplenty, soon joined by cello. There's really interesting use of chorded bass and piano later on. In fact, some of this made me think of hearing *Listen With Mother* on the wireless in the 1950s with my grandma.

The trademark arrangement is here, as is the oboe, which Robin seemed to flirt with before it quickly disappeared. His use of reeded instruments seemed to come and go. Mind you, double reed instruments can be a pain: the thin wood sometimes deciding to close mid-solo, so maybe he just got tired of all that.

'Through Horned Clouds' (Williamson)

Things pick up a step or two with another Robin trademark song, lyrics of mystical mystery, and instrumental sections, which sort of align with the rest of the song. I remember thinking that this was a very hard song back then, but now I think it's charming and not at all hard. Some of Robin's guitar playing echos the oud style. There is also more oboe. There appears to be a slight stumble about three and a half minutes in, but maybe 'it's only a northern song' and 'they just play it like that'.

'Sandy Land' (Williamson)

Side two's opener is as close to rocking as Robin gets. I mean, The Who wouldn't play on this. Drummer Gerry Conway does, though. Chugging piano, up-front bass and a moaning pedal steel make a rich sound for what is the most commercial track here. Funny that there's a line about smiles turned upside down that echoes a similar line on Mike's album: a piece of symmetry that suggests the two were still singing from the same hymn sheet after all. There's a nice middle eight – which is longer than eight bars – that keeps the beat without drifting off. And blow me down; the oboe is back too! Fab gear, baby.

'Cold Harbour' (Williamson)
This solo Robin acoustic guitar piece always seemed to me to be the album's quintessence: words that appear to mean everything without really understanding what's going on. It's the longest track here, clocking in at a little over seven minutes. If 'Warm Heart Pastry' seemed like Mike's future, 'Cold Harbour' certainly pointed the way to Robin's post-ISB work or at least some of it. I sometimes pass houses called Cold Harbour and think of this song, especially the section about halfway in, where there is a tract of low babbling voices. There's no way to work out what they are saying or even what language they speak in. It's mesmerizing.

'Dark Eyed Lady' (Williamson)
If there is a direct love song to Janet, this would be it. It's more acoustic Robin, with such a lovely melody and – just for a change – very easy lyrics. It's lovely. As they used to say at the time: ''Nuff said!'.

'Dark Dance' (Williamson)
A very short little instrumental of cello and oboe players. It's just an interval, but in its one-minute length, it is charming.

'I See Us All Get Home' (Williamson)
The album closes with a piano-led piece of hope that remained in Robin's repertoire through the solo years, even being re-recorded with a different title. Again there are straightforward lyrics and quite a sparse arrangement: above the piano, there's occasional organ and shimmering mandolins. I used to sit at home years ago, at the piano – the ISB *Second Songbook* in front of me – and happily play this.

Conclusion
So, there are the two solo efforts from the ISB days. In the final chapter, I'll mention some of the best post-ISB albums. These days, *Smiling Men With Bad Reputations* is easily obtainable, though sadly, at the time of writing, *Myrrh* is hard to find unless you fancy forking out over 30 quid on internet sites. It's strange that this was the cheaper album on release. You can read whatever you want into that costing imbalance.

After The String Band

So, what happened between 1974 and the late 1990s? After the String Band ended, Robin moved to America with Janet and formed The Merry Band, which would explore the Celtic side of his music, though initially, he wrote a number of quite Americana songs. The band was all tartan, bagpipes and harps, but was, as you might expect, damn good. It's worth seeking out the handful of albums they produced. Also, Robin increasingly took up storytelling, producing spoken-word cassettes of Celtic tales: and he was fantastic at it. Enthralling in live performance and engaging on record, his ability to act out the tales, was a revelation somewhat beyond his previous theatrical efforts. His solo albums were also quite Celtic-based, sprinkling traditional songs and tunes alongside matching original material. The song, 'For Mr Thomas', showed Robin's muse was still burning bright, and indeed, even Van Morrison covered that one. Robin made off-and-on connections, appearing as a duo with his wife Bina (which he does to this day), touring with Clive, Lawson and Bina, and working extensively with ex-Pentangle guitarist John Renbourn. After Janet and Robin's marriage ended, he moved back to the UK. He now lives in Cardiff and maintains a steady touring schedule as befits a man of his years.

Mike initially continued the ISB paths, forming the band, Reputation. Essentially it was the ISB without Robin, as it featured Mike and Malcolm, as well as John Gilston and Graham Forbes from those latter days. Their one album, *Reputation*, is one for the collectors, as it featured a couple of tracks destined for what would have been the next ISB album, and thus, Robin appears on it. It was on Melanie's Neighbourhood label and has a pretty decent line-up of guests, including Richard and Linda Thompson and Eddie Jobson of Roxy Music.

A solo album, simply titled *Mike Heron*, was recorded for the Casablanca label. Unfortunately, no sooner was the album pressed than the label went bankrupt, making the album now a very rare item in its original form.

Electric power was still in Mike's head as he and Malcolm became Heron: a bit of a rock band that nonetheless managed to bring forth excellent songwriting within one album, *Diamond of Dreams*. They were also pretty neat live, as I remember. Mike also managed to keep the coffers topped up through Manfred Mann's Earth Band managing sizable hits in other countries with Mike's songs: for example, 'Trim Up Your Love Light'.

Mike then disappeared out of sight – save for some Glen Row demo retrospectives – before re-emerging with a crisp little outfit called The Incredible Acoustic Band, who even got on TV when a drama about oil rigs featured a character who worshipped the ISB. As a special surprise, the other lads organised a party for him, with The Incredible Acoustic Band playing 'Log Cabin' and 'Everything's Fine'. Both songs featured in the bands live set, but primarily, they performed Mike's post-ISB repertoire. After the reformation folded, Mike continued – and continues – to play live with various people, including his daughter: a notable period being when he was backed by the rather lovely band, Trembling Bells. Mike has also written the first part of his autobiography, taking the story up to the start of *5000 Spirits*.

After parting with Mike, Malcolm continued to sing, being in The Enid for a while. He is back in Scotland now, largely spending his time performing in educational settings, singing of the virtues of fruit and veg, and promoting healthy eating amongst young people. He re-emerged into Stringdom when invited to the first String Band Convention in Hebden Bridge, Yorkshire, subsequent to which he produced a truly excellent album titled *Nothing Strange*.

After leaving the band, Rose was offered gigs playing bass for the likes of Steve Winwood. But with a view to becoming a studio engineer, she turned them down. Becoming an engineer never came to pass either, as marriage and children took over, and Rose ended up as Lady Mayoress of Aberystwyth. This caused a certain amount of press when the Woodstock festival anniversary loomed, as they couldn't resist headlines along the lines of 'Mayoress Who Played Woodstock In A See-Through Dress'.

Rose now lives in Devon, and after many years, has again taken up the fiddle, which had sat in its case, untouched since the day she left the ISB. Chiefly though, Rose has recently written her memoir of her years with the band, which was launched in late 2020. It's a wonderful read and captures the very essence of those hippie years for those of us who were there and explains it for those who weren't. If you have any interest in the ISB, then the book is essential. At the time of this writing, I await the second part of Mike's autobiography, as it will be interesting to compare the take on things from both sides of the couple.

Initially, Licky carried on performing in Scientology concerts but eventually faded from view. Her fate is unknown. Some say she has facts on the Scientologists that cannot be made public, and she is in hiding from the increasingly cult-like organisation. Others say she just wanted a quiet life and has tucked herself away in America. Others say she was last seen walking into the American desert and has passed away. Someday, perhaps the true fate of our darling Licky will be revealed.

After his brief sojourn with the ISB, Gerard Dott returned to working in the music shop and has also been spotted in trad jazz bands in Scotland.

Stan is back in America, though he popped up at the Edinburgh Festival in a trio with Malcolm, and Graham Forbes billed as Not The Incredible String Band. Graham continues to play and rock-climb and has written terrifically-entertaining books on both subjects. The two music books consist of reminiscences of life on the road, and being amongst the Rolling Stones tribute bands and such, have some interesting insights into the latter-day ISB.

Clive had a cult-like career after the ISB, with outfits such as Clive's Original Band (COB), but mostly lived a happy life making instruments, living in Cornwall and France. He produced some solo albums: in fact, I play sitar and percussion on one, though it was never released. After the ISB, Clive faded from view, passing away in 2014.

Other Albums You May Wish to Explore

So, since the band split(s), various extra things have emerged over the years, and it's worth flicking through some of them, as you may wish to explore them. Frustratingly, the band's Woodstock set was never made available in the film, nor on the triple and double albums that came and went; until, finally, the huge complete box set release, which contained the whole of the ISB set. Prior to this, some of the film had made its way out into the public, notably on a rather good ISB BBC documentary, which you can find on YouTube.

So, let's start with the live recording of the Bloomsbury 1997 concert, which I attended, along with a star-studded audience including Robert Plant and *The Old Grey Whistle Test* presenter, Mark Ellen. Although both Mike and Robin perform songs from their post-ISB years, there is a good scattering of the old stuff, largely arranged in new ways, not least because the Celtic harp has now become Robin's instrument of choice. But here is 'Everything's Fine Right Now', 'Red Hair', 'October Song', 'Maya', 'Koeeaddi There', '1968' (a lovely song of Mike's from the latter days, that never got released at the time), 'Feast Of Stephen', 'Log Cabin Home In The Sky', and the ISB live fave, 'You've Been A Friend To Me'. Mike and Robin are backed up by John Rutherford on guitar and Dave Haswell on brilliant percussion: both members of Mike's Incredible Acoustic Band. It's certainly a must-have for String heads.

An album of demos called *The Chelsea Sessions 1967* was released, which showcased the demos for *5000 Spirits*, including songs that never made it onto the album. All tracks date from 1967. The album opens with 'Mike's Lover Man', which never made the cut, despite being a pretty good little song. As is the next track – 'Robin's Born In Your Town' – which uses Robin's oud-style performance and wandering vocals and would have slid easily onto *The Hangman's Beautiful Daughter*. There's familiar ground next with a solo version of 'First Girl I Loved', sans Danny Thompson's bass. It remains one of the great songs of the period. Mike's 'Gently Tender' doesn't differ greatly from the final version with overdubbed flute and hand percussion. Much the same applies to 'Little Cloud', 'Blues For The Muse', 'The Eyes Of Fate' (or 'The Eyes Of Hate' as iTunes seems to call it!) and 'The Mad Hatter's Song'. They are fascinating steps along the way but don't differ greatly from the versions we all know. Robin's 'Alice Is A Long Time Gone' (a terrific little song) may be seen as a companion piece to 'The Mad Hatter's Song'. The ISB's history is littered with unreleased gems: 'Fine Fingered Hands' from the *Changing Horses* period is one case in point. 'Alice...' is gentle and sweetly rambling, while the following Robin song, 'See Your Face And Know You', sounds like *Wee Tam*-period writing: full of references to people of legend, over a finely-picked acoustic guitar and a few period-piece phrases. It's nice to have it here, but they had better material at the time. But not the next song – Mike's 'Frutch' – which is one of those comedy songs reminiscent of early Dylan, except it's not that funny. Its acoustic guitar and harmonica backing, though, is pleasant enough. Did we even need to know about a girl called Blit? Even in 1967?

'Iron Stone' appears in guitar form without the sitar but retains its simple beauty. 'God Dog' was a simple little song written by Robin, accompanied by Dolly Collins on the portative organ, providing a flute-like texture. Although the ISB never recorded it, Dolly and her sister, Shirley Collins, did take the song and place it on vinyl. This very straightforward love song to the canine is actually very beautiful.

The album finishes with a bonus track from 1968, which begins with Robin's 'All Too Much for Me', featuring Mike's organ and Robin's guitar. Ere long, they blend into two Blind Willie Johnson songs: 'Take Your Burden To The Lord' and 'Light From The Lighthouse'. Hey, even pre-Malcolm, there were lighthouses!

A very worthwhile release, you can now buy it as a double package called *The Circle Is Unbroken, Live and Studio 1967-1972*. The other half is a previously available live album recorded in Canada in 1972, featuring the Dott-period band. It opens with a driven version of 'Cousin Caterpillar' that totally rocks along with Gerard and Robin duetting: Gerard's clarinet on a new riff, driven along by drummer, Jack Ingram. Robin's up next with 'I Know That Man': an unreleased song that is more or less a blues, with Gerard swapping onto piano. It's familiar ground and style with 'The Circle Is Unbroken', retaining its organ and whistle setting, with Malcolm also playing whistle. It's not Robin's best vocal, it has to be said.

It's Gerard's showcase time as the band stray into trad jazz mode: Gerard leading on clarinet and Robin on mandolin. Next up is 'First Girl I Loved', but, oh dear, for whatever reason, Robin decided on a bossa nova arrangement, which really does not work in any way, as the melody is bent out of shape to fit. Best move on. It really is that weak.

'Everything's Fine Right Now' brings things back a little, with kazoo and mandolin, but 'Old Buccaneer' is as per the comments under *No Ruinous Feud*, though some of the lyrics differ and it's taken at a gentler trot. Next, Gerard is back to play some ragtime piano, with 'Catwalk Rag'. It's excellently played, and I'm a sucker for ragtime piano anyway. It's followed by Robin's 'Giles The Crocodile', which makes you wonder why it's here. As an amusing stage act, it was quite funny as I remember, with Malcolm taking the parts and dressing up. On record, at ten minutes long, it doesn't really work, but I suppose, for completists, it's available.

Then comes 'Turquoise Blue': still a lovely song and Janet here comes on stage to play flute. Gerard delivers a rather nice clarinet solo too. Next, Malcolm delivers a version of 'My Father Was A Lighthouse Keeper', with what sounds like keyboards taking the place of the original *Earthspan* strings. Apart from proving Jack was no match for Dave Mattacks, it's a strong version. 'Black Jack David' appears with clarinets and its David name.

Two bonus tracks end the album. Malcolm's unreleased studio recording, 'Oh Did I Love A Dream', sounds more like a demo than a live track. It's a fine song, though a close relative to 'The Actor'. The closing live track is a crowd-pleasing jig on the fiddle, called 'The Hag With The Money'. As it comes with *The Chelsea Sessions*, you can't complain too much, but it's hardly essential.

There are better subsequent live releases, particularly *Live at the Fillmore 1968*, which captures the band as a duo at the top of their game. 'Waltz Of The New Moon', 'You Get Brighter', 'A Very Cellular Song', 'October Song', 'Ducks On A Pond', 'Puppies', 'Chinese White' and 'Maya', are all present, as well as another 'you had to be there' track – where Robin gets members of the audience to ring bells – and a medley which starts with the traditional rhyme, 'A Pig Went A Walking' before Mike joins together 'See All The People', 'Swift As The Wind' and 'Mercy I Cry City'. An invaluable document.

Also worthy of your time is the double CD, *Tricks of the Senses – Rare and Unreleased Recordings – 1966-1972*. It spans the eras, with unreleased material, including Licky's song, 'Secret Temple', which was planned for *Earthspan*, I believe. Now that really is something that is an essential piece of the jigsaw, as are so many tracks on this well-researched album that really stands up fine in its own right.

If you want to see the band in action, there's very little out there. But check out YouTube for the surviving appearance on *The Julie Felix Show*. There is also a DVD called *The Lost Broadcasts*, which was shot in Europe and features live studio takes from the four-piece band. It opens with Irish jigs, before Rose and Lickyharmonise on 'Empty Pocket Blues'. Fun fact: Rose is wearing a pretty blue dress which actually belonged to Licky, who lent it to her. According to Rose, girly clothes-swapping was not usually a feature of their relationship. 'Everything Is Fine Right Now' has Mike doing some lead bass, and it ends with the short interview referred to earlier, where Robin speaks in French.

For the true aficionado, fans produced a set called *Gods Holiday*, which ran to some sixteen CDs, pulling in every radio session, outtake and utterance that could be tracked down. It's a mammoth work but is really only for the true fans who can bear to sit through low-fi recordings. It was only available as a vine network and was not for profit. A second set of live takes appeared later, making it even more mammoth. And yes, I do have it all.

The 21st Century Albums: Nebulous Nearnesses and Everything Is Fine

So, it kind of went like this. In a high profile interview, Joe Boyd intimated that Mike and Robin never really liked each other much: they were, as it were, work colleagues. Rose confirms in her book that the two would have tiffs, but who doesn't if they're so close to each other for so much time? Mike and Robin read the article and disagreed with the sentiment. Robin took to singing 'Painting Box' and 'Log Cabin Home In The Sky' in his concerts. And then strange things happened. They talked to each other on the phone and – so legend has it – even met up; Robin now white-haired and slightly rounded, and Mike, well, not much different to how he'd always looked really.

The comings and goings through the twenty-odd years since the String Band ended were given in the previous chapter. Now the big news was that they would do a handful of gigs together: some in London, some in Scotland. It was strictly to be billed as Robin Williamson and Mike Heron: not the Incredible String Band, and the outcome was the live *Bloomsbury 1997* album. Again, more details in the previous chapter. The shows went well, very well, in fact. The ISB back-catalogue on CD was selling very strongly indeed: a new generation having thrown off the shackles of the old 'the only good hippie is a dead hippie' routine, and, to cut a long story short, it was decided that the ISB would indeed reform. It would be Mike and Robin with Lawson Dando (mainly on keyboards) and Robin's wife Bina (mainly on vocals). Lawson had worked with Robin and Bina prior to the reformation. And, wait! Who was that thin chap on banjo? Yes, it was the return of Clive Palmer to Stringland, after all these years. Robin and Clive had been doing gigs together and recorded albums too. But instantly, fractures began showing. Robin wanted the band to press on with new material, while Mike felt there was a huge back-catalogue to explore. When I talked to Mike at the time, he pointed out that such was the pace of recording in the ISB heyday that no sooner had you toured in support of an album than the next one was recorded and the next tour was undertaken to support it. This meant that some of the much-loved classic material was left behind after scant live performance.

The new band debuted at Fairport's Cropredy Festival. I was there and thoroughly loved the whole set. But sadly, many of the audience declared them to be awful and possibly one of the worst acts at Cropredy ever. Far too harsh: the band had always maintained a degree of looseness, which added to their charm. Of the performance, one famous folk musician – who I shall not name – declared Robin as 'the consummate musical genius' and Mike as looking like 'he'd wandered onstage by mistake'. Again, grossly unfair. But then again, Mike was the one who hadn't toured constantly since the end of the original band. More of that, again, later.

Anyway, inevitably, Robin once again left the fold, taking Bina with him, which left Mike and Clive as the two remaining originals: which was strange, as they had hardly played together, Clive having been Robin's partner in crime before Mike was added. But, there was obviously a decision to continue on without Robin. Mike, Clive and Dando then recruited Clare Smith to fill the Robin and Bina roles, though Clare preferred to be known as Fluff. Fluff was primarily a violinist, but also played cello (including using it to impersonate a gimbri when required), recorders and mandolin, and sang. Thus, the 21st-century ISB was born.

There were two albums from this period, which I don't intend to analyze track by track, as neither contained new material, and both were live: in the case of the first one, sort of live.

Nebulous Nearnesses (2004)

Personnel:
Mike Heron: vocals, guitar, piano, organ, harmonica
Clive Palmer: vocals, five-string banjo, guitar
Lawson Dando: vocals, keyboards, 6 and 12 string guitars, thumb piano, kazoo, finger cymbals
Fluff: Vocals, violin, cello, mandolin, recorder, whistles, claves
With
Gavin Dickie: Bass and 12 string guitars, vocals
StieniGundmundsson: Tabla, darboukha, tambourine, triangle, guiro, woodblocks, shakers
Producer: Ben Findley
Record label: Amoeba
Release date: 27 April 2004
Running time: 1:01:46

The band wanted to have a controlled recording that would reflect well on them. So the studio chosen was Peter Gabriel's Real World, along with his producer, Ben Findley. Furthermore, the band would record it in front of a small invited studio audience. The material would be drawn from the back catalogue, though obviously weighted towards Mike's contributions, but not exclusively.

The album opens with 'You Know What You Could Be', followed by 'Cousin Caterpillar', 'Everything's Fine Right Now' and 'Chinese White'. There's certainly a magic in the performances: a mix of nostalgia and admiration for how well these songs had aged since those hippy-dippy days. Next, Robin gets his chance, as Clive leads a performance of 'Ducks On A Pond'. His performance lacked the magic of Robin's young vocal (whose voice wouldn't?), but it's a nice interpretation and a pleasure to find that Robin had not been erased from history.

After a run-through of 'How Happy I Am', it's then Fluff and Lawson's chance, as they basically duet on Robin's 'The Water Song', with the sound of Real World's mill stream mic'd in to provide the water sounds. It's actually a creditable job: keeping to the original feel, but at the same time, adding to it.

Clive follows with 'Banjo Tune': re-titled from its appearance on the first album, as befitting the more-enlightened times, but just as able to bring a smile to your face. Then it's 'Log Cabin Home In The Sky' and 'Painting Box': both terrific songs and performed here well. Clive is back in front with his own 'Empty Pocket Blues', Lawson's acoustic piano adding another dimension to a song that outlasted Clive in the band: still being performed in the four-piece with Rose and Licorice, years after. After a sprint through 'The Hedgehog's Song' with Lawson adding the slide parts, it's into the grand finale: A Very Cellular Song – which is remarkable in its recreation of the original, with Fluff high up the dusty end of the cello neck, sounding as much like a gimbri as it's possible to.

So, overall, if you love the songs and can't get enough, then you will be very happy with this album. Just don't expect it to be an indispensable part of the catalogue.

Everything's Fine (2004)

Personnel:
Mike Heron: vocals, guitars, keyboards, harmonica
Clive Palmer: vocals, five-string banjo, guitar, pipes, percussion
Lawson Dando: Vocals, keyboards, 6 and 12 string guitars, Indian harmonium, thumb piano, kazoo, finger cymbals
Fluff: Vocals, violin, cello, mandolin, recorder, whistle, percussion
Release date: 2004

The thing is, I'm unsure why this was released, as it so closely follows *Nebulous Nearnesses*, both in timescale and in repertoire. It's a live recording from The Lowry at Salford in September 2003. Yes, it's a double, so there are more songs. Yes, it's the audio from a DVD release of the concert, but I really don't know why. A single CD of the tracks not on *Nebulous Nearnesses* would have been fine, but then that would have omitted the classic tracks people would want. And of course, there are no session musicians on this one. The tracks appear in a different order but open with 'Everything's Fine Right Now', as before, though now moving to 'Ducks...' and 'Log Cabin...' straight after. But now we have a new track and the first to be plucked from the Island years. 'Maker Of Islands' is actually very beautiful in its live stripped-down form and very worthy of inclusion. We get more repeats with 'Banjo Tune', 'Empty Pocket', 'You Know What You Could Be' and 'Cousin Caterpillar', before CD 1 ends with a slightly rearranged version of the excellent 'This Moment', from *I Looked Up*.

CD 2 then duplicates again, with 'How Happy I Am', 'The Hedgehog's Song', 'The Water Song' and 'Chinese White', before surprising us all with a rendition of *Wee Tam*'s 'Douglas Traherne Harding'. Who would have thought Mike would be singing about people with no head in 2003? It's followed by the only track that is new to us all, featuring some instrumentals from Fluff on the fiddle and Clive on a set of pipes which he built himself. The tunes, for your information, are 'Cuckolds Away' and 'Because He Was A Bonnie Lad': a nice little addition, and in keeping with ISB tradition. Then it's back to Mike and the Island years, with a splendid rendition of 'Worlds They Rise and Fall' from *Liquid Acrobat As Regards The Air*. Then it's the set closer, 'A Very Cellular Song', but not the end of the CD, as 'Black Jack Davy' returns (complete with original spelling) as an encore.

So, if you're a completist, you have to have both albums, even though they duplicate so much. But if I had to choose, I would always go for *Everything's Fine*. Not because you get more, but because I actually prefer the performances on here, which sound more relaxed and spontaneous.

The Final Split
Any road up, the band once again split up. Though, to this day, Mike continues to base his sets on his ISB years, working with younger people for whom he is an icon, such as Trembling Bells. Robin remains true to himself, occasionally dipping into the ISB for his live numbers, also covering such unlikely acts as Motorhead, The Rolling Stones and Syd Barrett. Everything is fine right now, everyone.

Talking of the End, But We're All Still Here

So, there we are. The final bit. The band I loved for all those years, ever since that evening when I sat in the students bar at Bradford University and heard some students playing 'Log Cabin Home In The Sky', which saw me hooked: hooked and caught for life, in a mass of floating colour, exotic instrumentation and a network of fellow travellers. I saw them live, I bought their albums, even in the years when they were not so cool, and it took a lot of searching to even find the albums: in shops in Aberdeen and London, Cambridge and Halifax. There was a saga in itself. Bruce's Records in Scotland proved invaluable.

The *New Musical Express* had done a free magazine in which all the best bands were listed alongside their releases. Some ISB, I recognised, but, oh, the mystery of *I Looked Up* and *U*. What would my ears discover when I tracked 'them' down? I bought the songbooks so I could play the songs: the first one put together by Happy Traum, which told you where to put the capo and what tunings to use. Robin and Mike had little thumbnails of who they were at the start of the book. Robin told me that 'Everything is interesting in an infinite sort of way', and I took it to heart. I heard a story that, while organising the book, Happy had run over Robin's guitar: the Lowden with the hand-drawn illustrations, that was so iconic but disappeared. In later years, I discovered this wasn't the case and that Robin had had it maintained, and that involved the front being rubbed down and refinished.

I bought the compilation albums just for one track, and for the completists among you, there was *Relics* – which covered the Elektra years (a single album in the UK, a double in the US. Given the tracks were chronological, that was just plain weird! It's now readily available on CD) – and *Seasons They Change* (issued on Island but featuring Elektra material too). Crucially, it had the (then) unreleased track, 'Queen Juanita And Her Fisherman Lover': a track with more chuckles, this time from Robin, and featuring the only appearance of the conch shell in the instrumental roll call.

I was even – on paper – a member of the band for a few months in the 21st century. I was meant to tour the US with Mike and Clive, but my session with Clive – and our incompatibility – scuppered that. Ah well, at least it forced me to renew my passport.

And you know what? The music never ages. It remains as timeless and mystical as ever it did. I've met Mike and Robin many times over the years, met Malcolm, and sat in Rose's house playing fiddles with her. And that usually bursts the bubble of worship. But none of it ever did. Their musical achievements remain on the higher plane. And every time I play a concert or sit in a studio surrounded by my sitar, gdulka, Indian harmonium, shamisen and the other hundred or so instruments I play, the spirit of the ISB looks down upon me and informs my head and heart.

As a postscript, there are a few more words to say. As well as writing for music magazines over the years, I also have presented folk-based radio programmes for longer than I care to remember. In the course of that, you end up interviewing all manner of people, from Limahl from Kajagoogoo to Martin Carthy, from Ken Dodd to Dave Mattacks, and from steam locomotive drivers to knighted civil servants. And so, naturally, you seek out those you really want to speak to. That is largely what I do: have a conversation, not be an interrogator. It usually works, though Steve Harley took umbrage once. I meant no disrespect Steve, honest. And Fish was a wonderful chap.

Anyway, obviously, I sought out the much-beloved ISB members as it became possible, and armed with a Sony professional cassette recorder, and later a MiniDisc recorder – both with a good quality microphone – I would attend concerts and politely see if a few minutes could be spared before or after the performance. I can't remember now whether my first interview was Robin or Mike, but I think it was Robin. Robin is – as you would imagine – an excellent interviewee. He maintains that careful balance of answering your questions without going on and on and 'round the houses. It's been said that Robin is always very friendly and open but is often prone to tell you what he thinks you want to hear. This has never been my experience, I have to say, but maybe I never asked the awkward questions. As I recall, I never asked leading questions about the ISB, as it was said at the time that he wished to not play on that period of his life as he continued to move forward. Rather like Paul McCartney and The Beatles' songs, he now seems at home with the rich legacy that is his and is a little more open to things.

I first spoke to Mike when he was touring with his Incredible Acoustic Band. He had been out of the public gaze for a year or so, and my memory is that he sidestepped questions about what had brought in the bread during those years. And bear in mind, nobody was particularly rich: a lot of the accrued money from the halcyon days had found its way to the Scientology organisation, or so I am told. The first thing I noticed was Mike's huge and almost permanent grin. It was open and sunny, as befits an English teacher's son who escaped the office nine-to-five to bask in the wonder and magic of music. On that occasion, he had reason not to grin but still did. The venue – which I won't name – had organized a garden party in the band's honour, without telling them. The band rolled up and began to set up. When told about the event, Mike pointed out politely that they had been travelling and really only had the time to set up the gear and soundcheck. The 'management' took umbrage at this and stormed off in a huff, including the sound crew. Unperturbed, the band played on and were superb.

At this point, Mike was also less inclined to discuss the ISB years. He was not anti but simply keener to promote the IAB over the ISB. In later interviews – after the band's revival and demise – he was much more open about those years. Younger musicians were treating him like an icon. This status, he richly deserved and talked openly about the joy of playing his songs live, more than he had ever done in the ISB with the turnover of material in their nine-year span.

Rose was a whole new thing. Firstly it was on the phone. But Rose didn't have a phone, so she arranged to be at a house that did, at the appropriate time. Of the ISB interviews, she was the one that had me nervous before the event. Virtually every interviewee was pushing their new album or promoting a gig, but here was Rose with no agenda: only a history which I wasn't sure if she had out-of-bounds areas in. As it turns out, she was lovely: telling me openly that sometimes on stage, when Robin was getting people to ring handbells or the like, she felt embarrassed to be there. But the interview was all good, and after its radio broadcast, I duly transcribed it for a folk magazine. When I stayed with Rose for a few days, I avoided asking interview questions, but stories were offered, and I was delighted to drink it all in. Now with her book charmingly telling the story, you can share those moments.

Malcolm I chatted to briefly and was a little surprised by how shyly he came across. Here was the man who dressed as the god of the hunt, leaping over fields, or cavorted on the stage in crocodile mode. But maybe the years of being accused of being the beginning of the end had made him guarded.

Graham Forbes, on the other hand, was open and terrific to talk to. Having written books, he was not short of words and was happy to relate anecdotes of his time with the ISB in those final years.

Finally, my encounter with Clive was not successful. I wasn't there to interview him but to play on his album. He was full of a heavy cold and medicated. I think, simply, we didn't get on.

But what of live? I first saw the ISB live at The Great Western Festival, held at Bardney near Lincoln in 1972. It was the four-piece band of Mike, Robin, Licky and Malcolm. I went to the festival with work friends Arthur and Dave. Arthur maintained a constant fear that Hells Angels would attack him at any moment, and I gazed in wonder at these people gathered to hear music together. Thinking back, I have no recollection of where I slept, though a tent was surely involved, and I don't remember what I ate, or even if I ate at all. Ah, those heady days. The line-up was fantastic: The Strawbs, Faces, Sha Na Na, The Beach Boys, Rory Gallagher, and so many more. Even Slade, for goodness sake. John Peel introduced the acts and Monty Python did sketches between acts.

Anyway, come the time for the ISB, I knew little of what to expect, but Dave said, 'Listen to this chick's voice' (Look, it was 1972, okay?), so I did, and Licky melted my heart in seconds. What did they play? I really couldn't say, it was all new to me, but I loved them, and – along with other artists I was 'turned on to by the festival' – I was away on the love affair. If I was to guess the setlist, I could look at other festival appearances of the time: notably the rather soggy Bickershaw Festival, which Jeremy Beadle organised. I never thought there had been a connection between *Beadle's About* and the ISB, did you?

Other albums that I acquired following the festival, as you ask, included *Grave New World* by The Strawbs, *Henry The Human Fly* by Richard Thompson, and *Performance Rockin' the Fillmore* by Humble Pie. The first two are still regulars on my record-playing devices.

My next live ISB encounter was at Preston Guildhall, and I took my mum. I took her so I could tape the gig, and having a mum with you made you look less suspicious. I loaned the tape to someone who was writing a book on the ISB (which never appeared), and never got it back. If you're reading this, perhaps you could return it, sir.

Licky had gone, and Gerard had been and gone. I was more aware of the back catalogue, so I recognized 'Every Thing Is Fine Right Now' and a number of other pieces. 'Cold Days Of February' melted me with just Mike on Organ and Robin on whistle and vocals. Malcolm was an excellent frontman: dancing and leaping in the air and making almost surreal introductions throughout the set. 'Giles The Crocodile' gave us all a happy smile. Pronounced 'JeelsCrocodeel', Malcolm dressed up, and Robin spoke the words, prefacing the future storytelling that was to come. It ended – if I remember right – with jigs and reels and me trying not to look too interested in the females dancing vigorously in front of the stage, as my mum was sat next to me. Afterwards, at the sales stand, I bought a copy of *Liquid Acrobat As Regards The Air* and a poster. It was the one with the Gerard Dott version of the band and a wee dog sat on Mike's knee. If this was a band in its death throes, I would never have suspected so.

It would not be until the next century that I saw the band as the band again. There had been the Bloomsbury concert that I mentioned before, as it was recorded. I took my friend Jill with me. She preferred to be called The Pagan Space Cat, so that seemed appropriate. As I saw the band at Cropredy on their first reformed gig – with Mike and Robin together again – I delighted in it all. As I mentioned, others were less enthralled by it, to say the very least. But it was a big gig to debut at, and expectations were high. It was to be my only encounter of the band with Robin. The next version – with Fluff – I did see on a number of occasions and found them hugely enjoyable, despite the lack of Robin. The repertoire has already been mentioned in the two recordings from that period. In my heart of hearts, I always thought of it as Mike's band using the banner of the ISB, with Clive there for added validity. But still, the joy of hearing those songs live was palpable.

The post-ISB gigs began when I saw Robin at the Hebden Bridge Cinema in West Yorkshire. It was a mini-festival with few acts, including Northumbrian pipe player Alistair Anderson, of The High Level Ranters. He played a few tunes on the concertina during Robin's set. Robin had taken an earlier spot rather than closing the show so that he could catch the plane back to the USA, where he was still living at the time. I remember being slightly disappointed that his set was pretty much all traditional songs, nothing from the ISB repertoire, and precious little original material. It seems Robin was wiping the slate clean and going back to his roots. I still loved his set, though and was entranced by his rendition of 'The Parting Glass', performed on accordion, using only the chord buttons, I seem to remember. Incidentally, the opening act was a French woman with a banjo, who was obviously in an 'altered state'. She randomly hit the banjo and wailed in a manner that would have made Yoko Ono proud. She was dragged off the stage, protesting, and made further attempts to get back on through much of the evening before being removed from the building.

I continued to see Robin over the years, storytelling, solo, or with Clive, Dando and Bina, whatever loose line-up he used. But one gig I remember very well was attending the recording of a solo album which he had decided to do in front of a live audience. He did this at The Square Chapel in Halifax: an abandoned chapel which I had actually had a hand in saving from a crumbling destruction, leading to its resurrection as an arts centre and performance place. Robin had decided to record a selection of traditional songs using a brass band as backing, and where else would you go but the West Riding of Yorkshire for such a thing? As a gig, it was unusual in that songs would be halted in the middle and then restarted for recording purposes – Robin staying calm and jovial throughout the drawn-out process. The resulting album – *The New Fangled Tone* – is well worth seeking out, though I'm told that the young brass players had been somewhat lackadaisical in their preparation, considering it to be just some old folk singer they were playing with, and as a consequence, a fair amount of the brass parts had to be re-recorded. I have to say that on the night, this wasn't wholly noticeable, and the whole event summed up Robin's constant need to keep moving and find new avenues to explore.

Malcolm played at the Hebden Bridge ISB Convention (I know, Hebden Bridge keeps popping up, doesn't it?). His performance showed he had lost none of his showmanship, and he seemed genuinely moved by the warmth the audience showed him. When he played 'Down Before Cathay', the audience reacted and loved him more. From this concert came the impetus to record the fine *Nothing Strange* album.

Mike was the one you felt would have a more high-profile future after the ISB. The albums displayed a commercial FM-friendly approach that would take him further, we thought. My first live encounter with him was when Mike Heron's Reputation supported The Andy Fraser Band. Andy Fraser was the former bass player with Free, and my chief recollection of his set is that he played lead melodies on the bass all night, while the real bass lines came from the keyboard player's foot pedals. But I'd gone to see Mr Heron. I think I took a lady called Pam, but I may be wrong. Anyway, surprisingly, there was still a hint of ISB in the band: after all, it was still essentially the final line-up, minus Robin. Malcolm was there: still consummate in front of an audience, still the showman, even though Mike took most of the lead vocals. Malcolm had a featured spot involving dancing and a prop lamppost, called, perhaps, 'Street Light'. The repertoire, as you'd imagine, didn't touch the ISB, though there may have been some Mike's songs from the last days, that never got recorded.

I looked forward to more, but for a long time, that was it, as Mike disappeared from the limelight until The Incredible Acoustic Band appeared. The almost metal sound that had appeared had been left behind, and the new songs I first heard at Hebden Bridge Trades Club (yes, there again!) were lovely crafted items: 'Gaugin In The South Seas' being one example. There was also

'Log Cabin Home In The Sky' and 'Everything's Fine Right Now' to prove he'd come to terms with the past. The last time I saw Mike was at Sowerby Bridge Library: a small Victorian library with no stage. He was backed by Trembling Bells as they sat between the shelves of books and captured the magic of the early-ISB songs they performed. There was Mike's daughter on keyboards, and Mike himself looking so happy among the young players. Strangely, this felt more like the ISB than the reformed version had, and it was such a joy to hear 'Spirit Beautiful' and so much more from his astonishing back-catalogue, sounding so fresh and moving again.

As I write, the pandemic still holds us in its grip, so further live work is on hold, but I'm sure there is more left to enjoy from both Robin and Mike. Ladies and gentlemen of the band, I salute you for the way you enhanced my life, and no doubt that of many others too.

As mentioned before, to learn more from the horse's mouth, as it were, I would recommend as essential Mikes book, *You Know What You Could Be*: not only for his eye-witness account of those early years but for the second half of the book where Andrew Grieg not only gives insight into being in a duo in awe of the ISB but says a lot about Witchseason and how things worked in those pre-corporate days. Secondly, Rose Simpson's book, *Muse, Odalisque, Handmaiden*, is not only a truly wonderful read but looks out from the eye of the storm in a way that only a down-to-earth Yorkshire person can do. The final essential read is *Be Glad, The Compendium*. Currently out of print but still able to be bought, this thick volume contains the best of the articles from the *Be Glad* fanzine. For getting perfect views from all angles, and for trivia, it can't be beaten.

I hope you enjoyed this little tome and that you will pop back into it for years. I said at the beginning that its just my view, so please take it as read that your views are equally true. If you think 'Frutch', 'Bad Sadie Lee' and 'Weather the Storm' are the finest things they ever put on tape, who am I to argue?

So to all the Stringheads out there, brought back to invisible brethren-hood by Andy Roberts and Raymond Greenoaken of the *Be Glad* fanzine; to fellow music-creating followers who produced the tribute albums *The Hangman's Beautiful Granddaughter* and *Winged We Were*; and to those who painstakingly put together the massive *Gods Holiday* project, well, blessings on you all.

May Mike, Robin, Malcolm, Rose and all other ex-ISBers, continue to sing and play and may love surround them and you.

On Track series

Barclay James Harvest – Keith and Monica Domone 978-1-78952-067-5
The Beatles – Andrew Wild 978-1-78952-009-5
The Beatles Solo 1969-1980 – Andrew Wild 978-1-78952-030-9
Blue Oyster Cult – Jacob Holm-Lupo 978-1-78952-007-1
Kate Bush – Bill Thomas 978-1-78952-097-2
The Clash – Nick Assirati 978-1-78952-077-4
Crosby, Stills and Nash – Andrew Wild 978-1-78952-039-2
Deep Purple and Rainbow 1968-79 – Steve Pilkington 978-1-78952-002-6
Dire Straits – Andrew Wild 978-1-78952-044-6
Dream Theater – Jordan Blum 978-1-78952-050-7
Emerson Lake and Palmer – Mike Goode 978-1-78952-000-2
Fairport Convention – Kevan Furbank 978-1-78952-051-4
Genesis – Stuart MacFarlane 978-1-78952-005-7
Gentle Giant – Gary Steel 978-1-78952-058-3
Hawkwind – Duncan Harris 978-1-78952-052-1
Iron Maiden – Steve Pilkington 978-1-78952-061-3
Jethro Tull – Jordan Blum 978-1-78952-016-3
Elton John in the 1970s – Peter Kearns 978-1-78952-034-7
Gong – Kevan Furbank 978-1-78952-082-8
Iron Maiden – Steve Pilkington 978-1-78952-061-3
Judas Priest – John Tucker 978-1-78952-018-7
Kansas – Kevin Cummings 978-1-78952-057-6
Aimee Mann – Jez Rowden 978-1-78952-036-1
Joni Mitchell – Peter Kearns 978-1-78952-081-1
The Moody Blues – Geoffrey Feakes 978-1-78952-042-2
Mike Oldfield – Ryan Yard 978-1-78952-060-6
Queen – Andrew Wild 978-1-78952-003-3
Renaissance – David Detmer 978-1-78952-062-0
The Rolling Stones 1963-80 – Steve Pilkington 978-1-78952-017-0
Steely Dan – Jez Rowden 978-1-78952-043-9
Thin Lizzy – Graeme Stroud 978-1-78952-064-4
Toto – Jacob Holm-Lupo 978-1-78952-019-4
U2 – Eoghan Lyng 978-1-78952-078-1
UFO – Richard James 978-1-78952-073-6
The Who – Geoffrey Feakes 978-1-78952-076-7
Roy Wood and the Move – James R Turner 978-1-78952-008-8
Van Der Graaf Generator – Dan Coffey 978-1-78952-031-6
Yes – Stephen Lambe 978-1-78952-001-9
Frank Zappa 1966 to 1979 – Eric Benac 978-1-78952-033-0
10CC – Peter Kearns 978-1-78952-054-5

Decades Series
Pink Floyd In The 1970s – Georg Purvis 978-1-78952-072-9
Marillion in the 1980s – Nathaniel Webb 978-1-78952-065-1

On Screen series
Carry On… – Stephen Lambe 978-1-78952-004-0
David Cronenberg – Patrick Chapman 978-1-78952-071-2
Doctor Who: The David Tennant Years – Jamie Hailstone 978-1-78952-066-8
Monty Python – Steve Pilkington 978-1-78952-047-7
Seinfeld Seasons 1 to 5 – Stephen Lambe 978-1-78952-012-5

Other Books
Derek Taylor: For Your Radioactive Children – Andrew Darlington
978-1-78952-
Jon Anderson and the Warriors - the road to Yes – David Watkinson
978-1-78952-059-0
Tommy Bolin: In and Out of Deep Purple – Laura Shenton
978-1-78952-070-5
Maximum Darkness – Deke Leonard 978-1-78952-048-4
Maybe I Should've Stayed In Bed – Deke Leonard 978-1-78952-053-8
The Twang Dynasty – Deke Leonard 978-1-78952-049-1

and many more to come!